4150

THE CATHOLIC APPROACH

TO PROTESTANTISM

THE CATHOLIC APPROACH

TO PROTESTANTISM

GEORGE H. TAVARD
of the Augustinians of the Assumption

FOREWORD BY GEORGE N. SHUSTER

Translated from the French by the author

HARPER & BROTHERS, NEW YORK

This book is published in France
under the title of
A la Rencontre du Protestantisme

M5⸳ Ecumenical movement
Protestantism

Contents

Foreword

THIS unusually farsighted and profoundly spiritual book is concerned with matters about which people disagree, perhaps more vigorously than they do about anything else. Accordingly I shall begin my few words of introductory comment by stressing facts so evident that no debate concerning them seems likely to arise. They are contemporary facts. When during 1954 German Protestants living under Russian rule assembled in Leipzig 200,000 persons of all age groups for several days of recollection and earnest discussion, something happened which would no doubt have been impossible during earlier piping times of freedom. Nor was the ability of German Catholics to gather in like numbers in Berlin any less significant and novel. But when such events take place in an atmosphere not of confessional rivalry but rather of religious solidarity and friendship, something even more impressive has occurred. In all truth Europe had witnessed nothing like them since the close of the Middle Ages. Do they permit us to hope that the cleavages of Christendom can be surmounted?

Such meetings as these were not in any sense political rallies, and yet they have shown that religion is the final refuge of freedom. And in doing that they have also made manifest the truth that the ultimate dictatorship is not that of the proletariat, or of economics, but that of faith. The dictatorship of faith is, however, subtle and strange, because Divine Permanence and human impermanence are associated in it. What wonder, then, that the second should so often reveal its inadequacy? In days when it might have been possible to ward off the totalitarian tyrannies which have brought our world to so low a state of reasonableness and peace, religious men did not join for the spiritual victory which might have won for them all other things beside. Instead, immured in their several traditions, they eyed one another askance and so surrendered the priceless boon of unity to the enemies of their liberty. It was the disarray of Christendom which opened the gates and let down the drawbridges. And so it may well be true that the survival of the ideas and ideals which have given our society virtue and temper because they were rooted in Christian teaching and experience will depend on whether the union discussed in this book can be brought about.

After all the basic issue of contemporary civilization can be stated rather simply. What separates those who live in the light of religious faith from those who do not are radically antithetical concepts of time. If one holds that a man's life derives its meaning from what best serves the span of his creative years—the three or four decades during which he earns his livelihood, begets his children and makes his contribution, for good or ill, to the story of humanity—one may not illogically conclude that religion is at best peripheral and of concern only during those hours when there is nothing better for hand and head to do. But as soon as one says that these few years are transitory and only relatively important, that they have a prelude and an enduring sequel, one has no choice save to conclude that human achievement is as naught compared with human surrender to Him who alone can give to man's eternity a significance comprehensible in time. Now on this matter there is no difference of belief or attitude among Christians, and therewith a unity has been discerned which cannot be gainsaid, even if many other divergencies, superficial or profound, exist. In a time which like ours is so largely dominated by those who made the creative years of the individual the sole Absolute, the Christian challenge cannot be effective unless it be heard as one message despite the inevitable diversity of those who proclaim it.

Father George Tavard, who during many years of reflection and study has learned to know as much about the problem of reunion as any man could reasonably hope to, writes as a Catholic priest staunchly loyal to his Church and to the Papacy. He does not suggest that by making a few concessions all around, or by cutting off the roots from which every great religion draws its life, one can decree a sort of democratic federation of faiths each member of which would concede equality of stature to the others. Nor does he say on the other hand that since Protestantism is the result of secession from the parent Church during the sixteenth century all that can be done now is to wait until the process is somehow reversed. Instead he proposes an arduous and careful, a deeply believing and in the highest sense affectionate, interpenetration of Catholic and Protestant thought and experience. I hope it does no injustice to his complex and sensitive analysis of the problem to suggest that he pleads for the wholehearted dedication to the cause of reunion of spirits who elect to take upon themselves the heavy burden of channeling the manifold cross-currents of history into the one stream of service to the Divine Will.

This book does three things more, all of them memorable. First it reviews the history of what another has called the "scandal of Christendom" with a masterly objectivity. Why it was that believers parted company, and what as the centuries moved on the results of the parting have been, in terms of doctrine and culture; in what ways the desire for reunion emerged, and for what reasons it was again and again left unfulfilled; in what manner of men the urge to mitigate conflict became incarnate, and what lessons are to be derived from their experience—these are some of the themes on which Father Tavard comments with a scrupulous and often moving fidelity to the truth. Burckhardt's maxim that one does not study history to be cunning for a time but in order to be wise always has perhaps never been better exemplified.

Second, Father Tavard presents a theory of fundamental Catholic-Protestant divergence which seems an admirable starting point for discussion. The Protestant, he writes, regards the Church as a Communion which exists in its ideal state only in the world beyond. Here below individual Churches are associations of weak and often venal human beings. Sometimes they are closer to the transcending ideal than others come, and may be so adjudged. For the Catholic, however, his Church is the ideal become real; and though the men and women who comprise it may be imperfect and sometimes give scandal even in high places, they do not take from the *Una Sancta* (the one holy Church) its character as a Divinely willed institution. Father Tavard's theory is, to be sure, not a theme for abstract and barren discussion. It is rather a basis for evaluating actuality and for surmounting a negativisim which has no place for regard and charity.

Third, the book will bring to readers of English some awareness of what has already been accomplished in Europe. That since the close of the agonizing War many religious leaders and thinkers of undeniable stature have been concerned with the question of reunion and have indeed brought to genuine fruition new forms of Catholic-Protestant co-operation is too little known amongst us. Father Tavard offers both a succinct description of it and an evaluation which may, one thinks, have an appeal for many in this country, where the need for reunion has perhaps been less keenly felt even though the consequences of disunion have become more flagrantly evident with each new day.

When the reader has finished, he may not see that a goal devoutly to be wished has been brought much closer, but will unquestionably have been enabled to envisage that goal much more clearly and have been moved, if not to dedicate himself to the task, then at least to resolve that in his own person he will no longer form an obstacle to what in the final analysis we can only hope will be the healing waters of understanding and genuine affection.

GEORGE N. SHUSTER

Introduction

"ANYONE who is familiar with the inner development of
the Churches separated from us will admit the truth of the
following statement, that dogmatic differences—however
serious and important—are not today the main element
which hinders reunion. Much more important is the spiritual attitude on both sides." One of the great Catholic
apostles of Christian unity, Father Max Metzger, thus expressed in 1939 an idea that commonly prevails among the
Catholics who are concerned with the problems of divisions
among Christians. As found in most textbooks and as still
taught by professors with no firsthand experience in the
field of ecumenism, classical apologetics attempts a direct
refutation of the dogmatic positions of separated Christians
with weapons borrowed from the threefold armory of Scripture, tradition, and reason. This sort of apologetics is
soundly grounded in the Catholic certainty of adhering to
the fullness of Revelation. In a purely speculative realm
this ought to produce satisfactory results. For where they
go astray from the Catholic dogmatics, the Protestant positions indeed run foul of scriptural, traditional, or merely
rational points that a Christian theology cannot forego without weakening itself. Yet when we oppose a particular doctrine of the Separated Churches to a particular scriptural
quotation, a special traditional notion, or a rational judgment, we do not really hit the Protestant doctrine in question, precisely because the ground and the partial validity
of the latter do not lie in the field of abstract speculation,
but rather in the domain of experience.

This is why the genuine oppositions and the crucial parting points—whose meaning will be jointly perceived by the

mind and the heart—are to be sought for on the level of religious sensibility rather than on the level of faith. Before he comes to deny Catholic principles, a Protestant is simply a man who was born in a religious background other than ours. Before freely and knowingly accepting the sixteenth-century Reformation and the religious societies that date back to it, he has been influenced by a wide constellation of childhood impressions on which the very framework of his later thought has been patterned. He moves in a world where the great figures of the Reformation elicit respect and even admiration. For him religious history is not dated according to the development of a divine Church that lives through the centuries and unceasingly renews itself in the knowledge of Revelation. It is rather focused on prophetic personalities, similar to the seers of the Old Testament, that inspire enthusiasm for the Word of God. Far from being an institutional and sacramental structure, the Protestant spiritual environment is an existential dialectic whereby the Spirit makes himself known through a religious reading of the Bible. Faithful though he be to the community that has carried him in its arms since his first years, the Protestant Christian is nonetheless aware that this community is not an absolute. From day to day it evolves, tries to purify its religious outlook, to find in a sincere and faithful reading of the Holy Scriptures light for its hesitancies and doubts. The liturgical year, or what replaces it, makes little room for canonized saints. Rather it recalls the martyrs of the Reformation, the dead of St. Bartholomew's Day (August 24), or the victims of "bloody" Mary. Reformation Sunday (first in November) reminds him of Luther's nailing of his theses on the gates of the Castle's Church of Wittenberg. If he is French, the "feast of the desert" on the first Sunday in September evokes the Huguenot heroes. If he is English, he knows that November 5 is the anniversary of a Catholic plot against the British Parliament.[1] The

---

[1] Various historians have denied the existence of this plot, recently Hugh Ross Williamson, *The Gunpowder Plot.*

Church he frequents makes no attempt at mirroring the beauty of God with its architectural lines; on the contrary, its bareness inspires respect for His holy Word.

My next-door neighbor is a Protestant; and we live in different worlds. What we know of each other is one-sided or even false, disparaging if not hostile. How can we understand or know each other? According to the books where I read about him, his religious ancestors were schismatic, heretic, apostate, and sacrilegious. According to the books where he reads about me, my religious ancestors were corrupt and superstitious, idolaters and murderers. Should he read the books where I read about him, he would consider them filled with untruths and lies. Should I read the books where he reads about me, I would think them full of exaggerations and misunderstandings. Is it possible to span the chasm that separates us? For four centuries now we have been working side by side. Together we are born and we die. We study the same sciences and make similar discoveries. And for four centuries we have been prolonging the scandal that a divided Christendom exhibits to its own eyes and to those of the world.

This experience of a break within Christendom is commonplace in many countries. It evidently shows that nowadays Protestants and Catholics are kept alien to each other by religious sensibilities no less than by the quarrels of the sixteenth century. These were at the origin of our desynchronized reactions, and a knowledge of them is needed to understand our situation. They form the background for our oppositions. Yet they are no longer our oppositions as such. Before we reach the plane of dogmatic discussions, we therefore have to deaden the dangerous fire of personal or inherited antipathies, to overcome the itch that each feels at the religious ethos of the other, to end polemics inspired by mutual irritation rather than by Christian love.

When he faces the facts of Protestantism, the Catholic has to adopt an attitude. Which one?

The attitude that prevails in most quarters consists in

overlooking the situation of the Protestant man and focusing attention on that of the Protestant Churches. The problem is then shifted from the realm of human life to that of ecclesiastical politics. When this happens, the Protestant is considered not from the standpoint of the sincerity of his faith in Christ but from that of his membership in a non-Catholic religious society. And since the one Church cannot recognize any rival community, we then conclude that each Catholic must necessarily take each Protestant for an officially commissioned representative of a heretic body. The real problem, however, does not lie here at all. It belongs to the field of spiritual experience, of an experience of faith that is influenced by peculiar social conditions, ancestral customs, local traditions, and religious points of view.

The step to be taken first, therefore, consists not in condemning but in understanding. Not only the true sense of Protestant formulas and credal statements but their religious echo and their deeply human and Christian undertones have to be perceived. To acquire as though from the inside the "feel" of a situation to which we are strangers; to undergo, methodically yet with love, conditions of life and thought to which we are normally foreign and which reach to the depths of the religious soul—this experience is all the more exacting as it ever threatens to bruise our most profound convictions and hurt us in what we hold dearest of all: our allegiance to the Lord Jesus. Yet it is all the more purifying. It powerfully helps us to sift what is truly the Catholic faith and what is only a superadded turn of mind, what is our unfailing hope and what is a sentimental tie to transitory accidents entitled to respect in their very transiency. Provided he is equipped with a serious theology and a deep and serene conviction, the apostle who attempts such an experience does not walk on dangerous ground. There is no more danger than in every form of life, no more peril than in any other kind of apostolate. As a great apostle of the nineteenth century exclaimed "O cautious men, I suspect you thought Jesus Christ overbold, when he undermined the work of His Church by dying on the Cross . . ." (Emmanuel d'Alzon).

The second step consists in eliminating our own prejudices. History is radically ambiguous. Far from untying the twisted threads of the mind of man, it ties them into more and more hopeless knots. Whence so many outbursts of national pride or political arrogance as soon as the problem of Protestantism is mooted. Because the past saw religious wars and persecutions, because so many Protestants were killed by so many Catholics and so many Catholics by so many Protestants, because one nation is called Protestant and the other Catholic (while they are equally un-Christian), we all have inherited hatreds and distrusts which hinder fair judgment. Tragic as it is, it is a fact that popular Catholicism is not forceful enough to uproot the feelings of national pride that are woven into our religious dissensions and that feed them with poison. Patience is needed for human weaknesses, but it is too obvious that the various brands of nationalism have brought disaster on the prospects of an eventual reunion of Christendom—as though national prejudice, race hatreds that memory sharpens, had any title to wield influence over judgments of religious value. Yet facts are facts. And heroism is often required to escape those influences and unknot what time has so badly entangled.

The following pages outline the problem of Protestantism as it presents itself to a man who, over a number of years now, has tried to understand it with the help of both personal contact and theological reflection. The study of history, the requirements of Catholic thought, an appreciative acquaintance with Protestant thinking, and also—let us admit it—friendship have inspired these chapters. Their sole ambition is to contribute to build up what will deserve to be called a Catholic ecumenism, loyal to the demands of the truth and to the no less important requirements of love.

GEORGE H. TAVARD

The reader will be well advised not to attribute to the author the opinions of non-Catholic theologians that are mentioned in this book. The author adheres to the doctrine of the One, Holy, Catholic and Apostolic Roman Church as being the deposit of faith "once committed to the saints."

Part One

⇢⇢⟩⟨⟨⇠

POSITIONS

Chapter One

THE BEGINNINGS

THE first public action from which the Reformation may be dated took place on the eve of All Saints' Day, 1517: Martin Luther, an Augustinian friar who was Bible lecturer at the University of Wittenberg in Germany, posted at the door of the Castle's Church a now famous list of Latin propositions. In them he challenged the doctrine of indulgences such as it was preached by the Dominican John Tetzel. The origins of the Reformation, however, go much further back. Long before Luther there had been omens of a growing opposition between the temporal and the spiritual on the one hand, between the Christian spirit and some aspects of the ecclesiastical institution on the other: the priest John Huss of Bohemia, condemned to die by fire at the Council of Constance in 1415; the Oxford professor John Wycliffe, who died in 1385; the so-called "spiritual" party among Franciscans; the ever recurrent quarrels between princes and the Papacy, in Germany, France, and England, were pointers to a coming disruption. The theology that grew during the fourteenth and fifteenth centuries had a philosophical basis that marked a progressive lack of familiarity with the *fides quaerens intellectum* that had presided over the composition of "sentences," monographs, and summas in the great centuries of the Middle Ages. Toward the turn of the sixteenth century an increasing number of simoniacal prelates, of clerics living with concubines, of bishops who never resided in their dioceses pointed to the indifference and even the corruption of a sizable part of the clergy. Moreover, the nearly eighty-year-long Great Schism, when two, three, and even four claimants to the Papacy excommunicated one another, multiplied doubts and questionings as to the exact value of the Papacy as an institution. Many scholars and leaders, who were mainly interested in the unity of Christendom, toyed with the idea that a General Council may be above the Pope. And the humanist renaissance, especially in Italy, often went with a cult of religious paganism considered as equal, and perhaps superior, to Christianity.

When Pope Hadrian VI in 1522 sent his legate Chieregati to the Regensburg Diet, he sadly admitted, "We know full well that for many years detestable things have taken place near the Holy See. . . ."

Together with the general restlessness of mind of the period, such a state of things helps us to understand the mentality of an oversensitive friar in a small town of northeastern Germany. His exasperation at seeing holy souls bartered for money explains Luther's outbursts against indulgences, which forms a continuous text of ninety-five sentences rather than ninety-five different theses. Yet this would throw no light on his subsequent attitude if his theology, long before 1517, had not wandered outside the great currents of the Catholic tradition. Luther did not think out his conception of justification after he had left the Church, since he already taught it to his Wittenberg students in his Catholic years. His repudiation of Papal authority had been forecast in the conciliaristic ideas which he had shared, while still Catholic, with many of his contemporaries. His unbalanced conception of the transcendence of God proceeded to no little extent from the nominalist theology prevailing in the universities.

Yet one thing was proper to Martin Luther: he made "justification by faith" the core of Christianity. In patristic and medieval times Catholicism had been focused on faith in the Revelation of the living God in His Incarnate Son. As a result of what seems to have been a deep religious crisis in the years 1507-1511, Luther unwittingly upset the poise of tradition. Christianity became for him the *profound experiential awareness of being personally saved by Christ.* His commentaries on the Psalms and on St. Paul disclose this shift from a faith in Christ as reaching us in historical events and institutions to a faith in Christ reaching us in an inner experience of spiritual liberation.

Luther now feels released from his interior crisis. His sins remain, as also his temptations. He is a fervent priest, having without doubt his share of personal troubles, but knowing henceforth that no victory can come from his own efforts, his prayers, his mortifications, or the indulgences he may gain: he trusts only Christ the Savior. For the "just man lives by faith." In words that Luther was fond of, a Christian is "always sinning, always penitent, always just"— insofar as he believes in Christ, his personal Savior.

Had Luther alone been involved, he would have produced one more lopsided theology. The Church would have provided shelter to a new system, probably located next to the limit of orthodoxy. Communion with the universal church, however, would have gradually mended it. But Luther was not by himself. There were dissatisfied theologians. Among the aristocracy and the middle classes many angrily watched German gold filling up the treasure chest of an Italian Pope. A whole people waited and waited for a true reform of ecclesiastical mores.

The Wittenberg professor made news. His rising against the indulgence ordered by the Holy Father became known as quickly as news could then travel, and as it passed from mouth to mouth in cities, universities, and last but not least, convents and monasteries, it reached unexpected proportions. Overnight, and with no previous dream of it, Luther woke up a party leader. In 1518 at Augsburg, Cardinal Cajetan did his best to win Luther back to orthodoxy, with the only result that Luther appealed to the "future Council" in November, 1518. At Leipzig in 1519, while opposing the secular priest John Eck in a public discussion, Luther accused the Council of Constance of doctrinal errors in its condemnation of John Huss and affirmed that the authority of the Bishop of Rome could be traced back to Roman decrees less than 400 years old, which run contrary to Scripture and to the Council of Nicea.

Luther would have needed quiet and time for reflection. Meanwhile, however, the intellectuals grew more and more restless. A nobleman who was also a humanist and a writer, Ulrich von Hutten, had for a long time devoted his energies to spreading hatred for Rome. This was for him a golden occasion, and he wasted no time in urging Luther to open rebellion. Hurt as he was by the condemnation of his ideas by the famed universities of Paris, Cologne, and Louvain, Luther publicly burned, on Christmas, 1520, the bull *Exsurge Domine* by which Leo X had pronounced his excommunication. In that same year Luther had already, in his *Address to the Christian Nobility of the German Nation*, identified Rome with the "harlot of Babylon" and invited secular leaders to take in hand the reform of the Church. The bonfire of December, 1520, where the bull and the volumes of Canon Law were reduced to ashes started a conflagration that has not yet been put out.

A few pages would not suffice for a survey of the works of Luther or of his heroic fights against the most radical of his followers. "His gospel" as he understood it justified neither the peasants' revolt nor the spiritual anarchy of the Anabaptists; it did not countenance immorality or the rejection of sacramental realism. Though he recognized no more than two sacraments—baptism and the Eucharist— Luther practiced confession all his life. In spite of his outbursts of scurrilous language, Luther ranks among the most delicate devotional writers with his essay on *Christian Liberty* (1520) and his very devout commentary on Mary's *Magnificat* (1521). The main work of his life, in which the soul of Luther is best revealed and which deserves to remain a monument to his genius, is no other than his outstanding German translation of the Bible. Started in 1521, it was ended only in 1535 and Luther revised it until the end of his life. What he aimed at in this work was an intimate contact with the Lord: he wanted to make Him a living and as it were always contemporaneous figure. His readers would thus share in his faith of being saved by Christ and would be freed from the ecclesiastical contrivances of Rome, which the devil—as he thought—had invented.

It would be unfair to judge Luther only on the abuse he freely heaped upon his enemies (after all, neither St. Jerome nor St. Bernard was truly respectful of his adversaries); his Catholic contemporaries reciprocated quite openly. His marriage in 1525 with Catherine von Bora, a nun who had stolen away from her nunnery to be loyal to her Lutheran convictions, was in no way, contrary to what some have believed, a motive of his revolt. The Dominican Bucer, the Canon and Archdeacon Carlstadt, monks and nuns of all orders had entered wedlock long before Luther ever thought of it as a possibility for himself. His true personality is to be sought for in his deep piety, which was medieval rather than modern. He never could understand the radicalism of Zwingli, the Swiss Reformer, or the logical sternness of the Frenchman Calvin. What he was concerned with above all consisted in day by day discerning in Scripture the Word of salvation which was at the center of his thought and experience. Once he had perceived it in a text of the Psalms or of St. Paul—his favorite books—he could not question the wisdom of his titanic fight with what he thought were false forms of piety. Luther's tragedy is that true piety never warrants theological orthodoxy, and that a sound formulation of faith among his Roman foes did not always go hand in hand with a real concern for things of the spirit.

When Luther died at age sixty-three on February 18, 1546, half of Germany and the whole of Scandinavia had turned Lutheran; a great part of Switzerland had followed Zwingli or Calvin into heresy; France was undermined by Calvinism; England, schismatic for twelve years by then, was badly equipped to stem the spread of the new ideas; Scotland led a flirt with antipapism. And the Council of Trent, now two months old, came too late to prevent the split of Christendom into rival factions.

Many strong personalities arose during the sixteenth-century crisis. Since we have to make a selection, we now must mention a man without whose influence modern Protestantism would be very different from what it is: for if the Protestant Churches originated in the powerful Lutheran break-through, most of them owe their theology to John Calvin.

Calvin is before all else a thinker. When he was, probably in 1534, won over to the new ideas by what he called later a "sudden conversion," he was converted to a life of theological study. Calvin was a scholarly humanist who had written a commentary on Seneca. Well versed in Roman Law and initiated to Hebrew he had devoted his life to fashionable humanistic studies after giving up the idea of an ecclesiastical career. Dominated by Lefèvre d'Etaples, French humanism had a religious orientation, and Calvin was himself, as he puts it, "stubbornly given over to the superstitions of the Papacy." His "sudden conversion," following no doubt an unconscious preparation, oriented Calvin toward a deeper and more systematic study of the new doctrine than had been attempted so far. He seems to have started work right away on what was due to become his main contribution: a book which he rewrote time and time again, which he constantly revised and polished, edition after edition, on the *Institutes of the Christian Religion*. The theological works of Calvin now adhering to the Reformation had also a pedagogical and propaganda value. As they appeared for the first time in 1536 at Basle, the *Institutes* largely followed the plan of the catechisms of Luther and Bucer. It was an unsigned work, written in Latin and dedicated to Francis I, King of France.

Being a writer by vocation and taste, Calvin would have liked to spend his life among books. Yet, against his wish, he accepted care of souls. The city of Geneva had chosen the Reformation for political expediency rather than by conviction. A French Reformer, William Farel, was having a hard time trying to impart his beliefs to the Genevese. He insisted so much that Calvin finally yielded and replaced him in Geneva in 1536. Two years later the opposition drove him out of the city and Calvin spent fruitful years in Strasbourg with the Reformer Bucer. Geneva called him back in 1541 and he stayed there till his death on May 27, 1564.

Although Calvin adopted the thought of Luther on many points, he was far from being converted simply to Lutheranism. On some essential points—as for instance on the Eucharist—he definitely overstepped the German Reformer. What does seem to provide the basis of Calvin's view of "the true religion" is not indeed the celebrated doctrine of predestination, which was not even mentioned in the original edition of the *Institutes*; it is rather a peculiar understanding of Scripture as the Word of God.

Far from thinking, like Luther, that Scripture is clear, Calvin, a scholar who has pored over texts, knows that it is hard to understand. Since it is God's work, the human mind is not fitted to master it. To that end it must be directed "to the point where the Holy Spirit calls it" (*Opusc.*, 3, xxiii). Only by yielding to the "interior testimony of the Holy Spirit," to His "secret operation," to the "light of God," can one obtain the key to the Scriptures.

As Calvin explains it, this "secret operation" coincides with justification: "By no vain speculation can one know the holy and spiritual union which is between Him and ourselves and again between Him and His Father, but this is the holy means of knowledge, when He pours out His life in us through the hidden virtue of His Spirit" (*Comm. John*, xiv, 20). And elsewhere: "This communication of Jesus Christ . . . is offered in the Gospel" (*Inst.*, iii, I, 1). The very core of Calvin's thought lies in this conjunction of Scripture as the Word of God with the "hidden virtue of the Holy Spirit."

Calvin's evangelism, much more radical than that of Luther, follows from that premise. His insistence on predestination explains why so many are not acquainted with the Gospel. Calvin stresses the "horrible majesty" of God, who grants or denies knowledge and life through irreformable decrees. Yet this emphasis goes with a steadfast hope, expressed in the words of Calvin before his death: "Lord, Thou crushest me, but I am satisfied since it is Thine own hand."

One may gather from the posterior development of Protestantism that when Calvinism does not make predestination to heaven or to hell the focal point of its doctrine it is more universally attractive than Lutheranism. The humanism of its origin, its independence from political powers (which by no means entails a refusal to use violence), a rare concern for the laity, which transforms every employment into a divine calling, the earnestness of its ethical requirements—all this insured its success in areas where the Lutheran experience of justification found little echo. Yet Calvinism quickly became a nursery of sects. At least at the beginning, the Lutheran institutional framework was conservative to no small extent and counterweighted the subjective elements of Luther's doctrine. These are, on the contrary, emphasized by insistence on the "interior testimony of the Holy Spirit." In Calvin's teaching, this interior testimony does bear, not only, as Luther would have thought, on the doctrine of justification, but furthermore on all the contents of the Bible considered as a divine oracle. This entails, in the first place, a legalistic tendency, which is carried to an extreme in the "fundamentalist" sections of American Protestantism. In the second place, illuminism finds favorable ground when the testimony of the Spirit is mistaken for an infallible individual inspiration. Calvinism thus contained the seeds of the future multiplication of sects.

Whereas Lutheranism is to be found in strength in Germanic countries only, where it has even been dyed, to a certain extent, with Calvinist elements, Calvinism grew in France, Switzerland, the Low Countries, and Scotland. The Protestant orientation of the Church of England under Edward VI and Elizabeth reflected its main influence. It also held more sway than any other religious doctrine or practice over the development of the Protestant atmosphere of the United States of America.

Before surveying the present extension of Protestantism, a few words ought to be said concerning the Anglican communion.

As against the continental Reformation, the English Reformation originated in no outstanding religious personality and created no new doctrinal system. The quarrel between King Henry VIII and Popes Clement VII and Paul III was primarily motivated by political aims more than by theological doctrines or canonical scruples. When he forced Parliament to proclaim him "Supreme Head" of the Church of England in November, 1534, Henry himself had in mind no more than a reform of the political aspect of ecclesiastical institutions and intended to remain, for everything else, a defender of Catholic orthodoxy. Under the child-king Edward VI, however, the Archbishop of Canterbury, Cranmer, unified the rites of worship with his famous *Book of Common Prayer*, which an Act of Parliament imposed on all dioceses in England in January, 1549. Cranmer's moderately conservative demeanor concealed Lutheran convictions. The Prayer Book that he produced blends Catholic texts, open to Lutheran or even Calvinist interpretations, with omissions that leave hardly any doubt on Cranmer's basic Protestantism. The whole is, admittedly, unified by an undeniable liturgical talent. Owing to the Prayer Book, the Anglican communion is an ecclesiastical establishment centered on worship rather than on the Bible or on doctrinal tradition. The term "Protestant" or the adjective "Catholic" can fit it only with important qualifications. This enables Anglicans to use either or both with perfect sincerity.

After a short Catholic restoration under Mary Tudor (1553-1558), Elizabeth, who was less interested in religion than in the cohesion of her kingdom, established by law a moderate form of Protestantism. The Thirty-Nine Articles were adopted in 1562 as the doctrinal framework of the Church of England. They display a clearly marked Calvinist influence, even though some theologians have provided them with Catholic-minded interpretations. But the Queen was content with exterior conformity. Assisted by undistinguished prelates, she did not impose, with her reform of doctrines, a reform of behavior. Thanks to the Elizabethan settlement, the English Establishment became Reformed as to its liturgical texts and doctrinal formulas, while it remained unreformed as to its moral and spiritual life.

The upshot of this has been that the Anglican Church suffers from a radical ambiguity. The efforts of its Protestant-minded members and the endeavors of its Catholicizing sections have both failed so far to free it from the unresolved conflict consequent upon that equivocal origin.

Chapter Two

THE CHURCHES

THE origin of the Protestant Churches does not explain all in modern Protestantism. One has also to be acquainted with the developments posterior to the Reformation. Since such a study would, however, overflow the limits of the present book, we will restrict ourself to an outline of the main Churches such as they now exist, after an evolution that can only just be pointed out.[1]

THE LUTHERAN CHURCHES

As solemnly agreed upon at the Peace of Augsburg in 1555, the Princes of the Holy Empire could impose on their subjects the religion of their choice. This had been the tacitly accepted policy since the Diet of Speyer in 1526. At the origin the Lutheran Churches were therefore State establishments. In a number of States the Church officially became Lutheran. This took place in several parts of Germany and in the Scandinavian countries. Lutheranism adopted another status in the countries where it mustered only a minority of the people. It also altered some of its

[1] It is well to distinguish between "denomination" and "church." The church is an organizational unit. The denomination is a doctrinal tendency or tradition that may be common to various churches. Thus, Presbyterianism would form one denomination, but there are a number of independent Presbyterian Churches.

ways when emigration introduced it in America. Only the Scandinavian countries still now maintain the principle of the State Church, Germany having discarded it officially with the Constitution of the Weimar Republic and emotionally under the Nazi persecution.

Traces of that origin nevertheless mark German Lutheranism. For Germany knows of three sorts of Churches that may be called Lutheran. Thirteen are strictly territorial, eleven of them associated in a Federation of Lutheran Churches in Germany (VELKD). Ten territorial Churches are "united," having parishes of both Lutheran and Calvinist persuasion, the Lutheran being usually in the majority. (This union was imposed in 1817 by Frederic William III of Prussia.) A few other Churches are "free," having severed themselves from the State Churches. Most are grouped in a federation of "Evangelical Churches in Germany" (EKD), which is opened to non-Lutherans.

Like the Scandinavian Churches, those of Germany have kept on a number of points the externals of Catholicism. The title and function of Bishop—though not the episcopal succession in the sacramental sense of the words—the frequent use of Catholic liturgical vestments, the material setting of the old medieval churches endow European Lutheranism with a rather conservative organization and form of worship. Its general stand by the Catechisms of Luther and the Confession of Augsburg—written by Philipp Melanchthon to be used at the Diet of Augsburg in 1530 and stressing points of contact or kinship with Catholicism—extends this conservative tendency to the realm of doctrine. In spite of crises of liberalism in the last two centuries, the Lutheran Churches thus form the most stable section of modern Protestantism.

One may wonder if the most powerful Lutheranism is nowadays to be met with in Europe or in the United States of America. Dating back to the eighteenth century, when German or Scandinavian settlers came to the New World, American Lutheranism presents specific features. There are neither territorial Churches nor Bishops. Instead, a number of "synods" or Churches are constituted on a broadly democratic basis. Isolated at first by the immense distances of the American territory, they underwent reshuffling processes provoked by geographical location or a common national origin, or motivated by similar doctrinal emphases or customs. The sixteen Lutheran Churches of the United States form two distinct groups, the "National Lutheran Council" and the "Synodical Conference." The former is affiliated to the "World Lutheran Federation," of which the latter keeps clear. Most of those Churches result from past mergers or envisage possible future unions. One of them, the Missouri Synod, has, however, traveled alone since its formation in 1847. It now constitutes the most powerful single Lutheran Church of the United States, with nearly 2,000,000 faithful. Its insistence on doctrinal integrity, on classical Christian ethics, and on parochial life renders it neighborly to some Catholic forms of life. At the same time it also opposes more self-consciously and outspokenly than others the Catholic doctrine of the Papacy.

Outside of these great Lutheran communities, we may mention smaller groups, the most bulky ones being in Hungary, France, Austria, and South America. Finally, the missionary effort of the nineteenth and twentieth centuries has resulted in the growth of Lutheran minorities in Asia, Africa, and Australasia, totaling some 2,200,000 baptized members.

Most Lutheran Churches have since 1947 been joined in a "World Lutheran Federation," inside of which each Church remains independent. There are altogether approximately 68,500,000 Lutherans, of whom 30,000,000 are in Germany and nearly 7,000,000 in the United States.[2]

[2] These and subsequent figures come from a comparison of the statistics given in several books: *The Lutheran Churches of the World*, 1952; *Yearbook of American Churches*, 1955; *The World Christian Handbook*, 1952; F. S. Mead, *Handbook of Denominations in the United States*, 1951; V. Ferm, *The American Church of the Protestant Heritage*, 1953.

THE CALVINIST HERITAGE

As against the Lutheran tradition, the Calvinist heritage is maintained today in Churches whose origin is not always connected with the Reform of John Calvin. Besides the properly Calvinist French-speaking Churches of France and Switzerland and the Kirk of Scotland, founded by Calvin's disciple John Knox, Calvinism penetrated at an early date in German and Dutch territories that had formerly been Lutheran; its influence in England gave rise to the English "free Churches" and, as a consequence, to the most powerful branch of American Protestantism. Calvinism is nevertheless no denomination as such; it is rather a spiritual atmosphere that pervades several denominations.

Roughly speaking, these Calvinist denominations are called "Reformed" in continental Europe, "Presbyterian" or "Congregationalist" in Great Britain and America. Their organization is definitely presbyterian. Episcopacy is considered unnecessary. The apostolic succession is claimed as being that of the "true doctrine" taught by the preachers of the Reformation. The word "presbyterian" in this case does not refer to the Eucharistic priesthood, in which Calvin disbelieved, but to the institution of "presbyters" or elders entrusted with the management of the churches, the minister being only a qualified preacher who presides over the council of elders in the parish. A federation of local churches forms a synod or consistory where delegates from the laity sit on equal terms with delegates from the ministers. Since the French Huguenots adopted in 1559 the presbyterian form of government as well as Calvinist formulas of faith, doctrinal Calvinism is joined to presbyterian administration in the European *Reformed Churches*.

In many cases this doctrinal Calvinism has lost some of its original edge. Calvin's thought on predestination is often overlooked. The austerity of Calvinism, its legalistic emphasis on the will of God as expressed in the moral laws of the Old and the New Testament, occasionally gave rise to extremes, as happened in the puritanism of seventeenth-century England. Although, on the whole, puritanism has now been reduced to a latent existence, the English puritans provided the *Presbyterian Churches* of the Anglo-Saxon world with their five fundamental books, the *Confession of Faith,* the *Directory of Worship,* the two Catechisms, and the *Form of Government* adopted by the Westminster Assembly in 1643-1648. The growth of Presbyterianism in the United States is due to a great extent to the "Great Revival" which swept through most American states at the beginning of the eighteenth century.

As for the *Congregational Churches,* their origin and doctrinal basis are the same and they also made headway thanks to the Great Revival. The main difference belongs to the administrative order, each parish being all but entirely independent. Many Congregationalist pulpits have, however, lost contact with Calvin's theology, which has often been replaced by a "social gospel" largely diluted in sentimental religion.

The same remark may apply to the *Baptist Churches.* Historians disagree as to their origin, some tracing it back to Anabaptist groups in the Netherlands of the sixteenth century, others finding it in the Calvinist influence on seventeenth-century England. At the present time the only doctrinal bond of the Baptist Churches is the principle of "faith baptism," given only to adults who explicitly profess the Christian faith. Outside of this the teaching may range from the ultra-Calvinism of the "Old School Baptists" (6,000 in the South and West of the United States) to the pelagianism of the "Free Will Baptists" (40,000 in the United States). Some do not recognize baptism as valid when it has not been administered by a Baptist. In the main, therefore, a great variety of opinion is to be found and some Baptists have hardly anything in common with some others. The "Southern Baptists," with 8,000,000 adult white Americans and nearly all Negro Baptists (7,000,000 adults), form a group that was formerly—since the Civil War—sharply distinguished from the "Northern Baptists." Like several other Southern groups, they kept longer the forms of religion that had flourished in the frontier settlements when the pioneers were impatient with, or ignorant of, or simply unable to insure, institutional forms of worship. At the present time, however, the extreme forms of revivalism and fundamentalism—the two plagues that spread where ignorance goes with fervor—characterize newly arrived religious groups much more than they do the Southern Baptists.

The *World Christian Handbook* for 1952 gives a total of 41,100,000 for the Reformed and Presbyterian Churches, and 5,000,000 for the Congregationalists. The Baptist groups have 18,000,000 baptized adults (or some 40,000,000 members), of whom 16,000,000 are in the United States.

THE ANGLICAN COMMUNION

The modern Anglican communion is a vast fellowship of Churches that branched off from the Church of England or that have a similar origin. They are united together, symbolically by their communion with the See of Canterbury, really by their allegiance to the *Book of Common Prayer* adapted to the uses of different countries and lands, and organically by their episcopal structure. It would not be within our topic to discuss here the historical ground for Pope Leo XIII's decision to declare Anglican orders invalid and the corresponding episcopal succession fallacious, whereas Anglicans maintain that they have faithfully preserved episcopacy as it existed in England before the Reformation. Our description must, however, respect the "catholic" conscience of Anglicanism, even though our own judgment may attribute another value to the same terms or facts.

The Church of England itself, once it had become schismatic, yielded to influences that must be called heretic. Yet it has carefully protected its original structure. According to the Elizabethan settlement of 1562 and the 1662 Restoration after Cromwell's Puritan Commonwealth, Anglican Bishops in England are nominated by the Crown. Yet although the King or Queen bears the title of "Supreme Protector" of the Church of England, and although this Church is by law established as the Church of the Nation, its government is autonomous to a great extent. The Convocations of Canterbury and York—the two Archbishoprics —where delegates of the clergy and the laity gather in an Upper and a Lower House, carry legislation for their respective areas. The "Church Assembly," comprising delegates from the two Convocations, is the supreme governing body. The principle stands that some decisions must be ratified by Parliament before they become law, yet the Church Assembly and the Convocations are competent for everything that can be called a ruling instead of a law.

Two other sorts of Churches also make up the Anglican communion. Some, like the Episcopal Churches of Scotland, Wales, and Ireland, have an origin similar to that of the Church of England. The others are upshoots from one of these. The most important is the Protestant Episcopal Church of the United States. Others are the Churches of Canada, Australia and Tasmania, New Zealand, South Africa. There are, furthermore, missionary dioceses in various parts of the world. In 1948 the Anglican communion totaled 430 dioceses with an approximate 30,000,000 baptized faithful and 9,000,000 regular communicants. Every ten years or so the Lambeth Conference gathers the Bishops and provides them with an opportunity to publish a common pastoral letter and confer on their problems.

The Anglican communion presents itself as a commonwealth of Churches united in prayer, since all find their inspiration in the liturgical achievements of Cranmer. As distinguished from the Protestant Churches, it is not tied down to any particular doctrine of the Reformation. The official doctrine is no other than the implied contents of the *Book of Common Prayer,* which were formulated for their era in the Thirty-Nine Articles of 1562. The Prayer Book, in spite of its undoubted liturgical genius, remains theologically ambiguous. The Thirty-Nine Articles have clearly Protestant overtones. Because of their narrow historical background, however, they now represent an antiquated formulation and they cannot claim normative value at the present time. The official documents embodying Anglican doctrine are therefore open to a progressively enlarging interpretation analogous to a doctrinal development.

In its classical form, Anglican theology derives from the English divines of the seventeenth century, for whom both continental Protestants and "Papists" were tainted with heresy. Practically unaffected by the hardening which followed the Council of Trent among continental Protestants and the Catholics of the Counter Reformation, they upheld as the Christian ideal a moderate Catholicism where purity of evangelical preaching would go hand in hand with a patristic and even medieval theological culture. The subjection of the Church to the State was only for them the legalization of a state of things that had been all but universal in the Middle Ages. What they objected to in "Papism" was not the Catholicism of the great theologians but precisely what is meant by the word itself: the obedience of all episcopal sees to one of them, the claims of one to lord it over all, and, accordingly, the liturgical and doctrinal elements which they thought, with a questionable acquaintance with history, derived from a papal pressure on medieval Christendom.

This interpretation of "catholicity" provides a key to

what is now called "High Church": it is the movement of thought and the liturgical practices which have maintained and developed the conceptions of the seventeenth-century divines. The "Low Church" movement, which coexists with it, goes back to the Protestant influence under which various sections left the Anglican Church to form the English free Churches. In its present form it is largely marked by the evangelical revival that stirred the Church of England after the Methodist reaction at the end of the eighteenth century. A "Broad Church" movement, of lesser importance, must also be mentioned: it shows affinities with the theology of F. D. Maurice in the last century, yet much more than the deeply religious thought of Maurice, it perpetuates a nonreligious liberalism or skepticism. As for what is called "Anglo-Catholicism," it is the section of High-Church theology that has, since the heyday of the Oxford movement, developed a more and more Catholic-minded interpretation of Anglicanism: it is the Oxford movement such as it survives itself within the Anglican communion.

These four theological tendencies coexist and influence one another. Their peaceful dwelling together makes the vast Anglican abode a shelter of all theologies and an unstable synthesis of all the divisions and all the unions of Christians.

THE METHODIST MOVEMENT

Incipient Methodism was a religious revival in the Anglican Church. John Wesley (1703-1791) reacted to the indifference and practical materialism of a large part of the Anglican clergy of his time and attempted a return to the Gospel which would have, as he saw it, reformed the ethos of the Church of England. His success cannot be doubted. For the evangelism that spread to most Anglican pulpits toward the turn of the nineteenth century may be traced back to Methodist emulation. After his death, however, the "Methodist conferences" that he had established in the course of a life filled with apostolic labors of hardly comparable extent, decided to break with a Church which did not look upon them with favor. The Methodist Church is thus one of the Churches that are called "free," that is, free from the guardianship of the British State and the influence of the official Establishment.

Governed by yearly conferences—of which there are 119 for the United States alone—Methodism has borrowed from the Church of England the main elements of its worship. Its cult—where it is still practiced—is therefore a streamlining of the rites of the *Book of Common Prayer.* The Twenty-Five Articles of religion that provide the framework of its doctrine are excerpted from the Elizabethan Articles. Yet one cannot speak of an official doctrine without qualifications. For Wesley intended to deny admittance to nobody on doctrinal grounds. Provided that he adheres to the Book (the Bible), that he wants to remain faithful to the "testimony" of the Holy Spirit (conceived as a call to holiness rather than as Calvin's interior illumination of faith), that he focuses all his life on the experience of conversion, anybody may join Methodism. No acceptance of a specific doctrine is required, although the Methodist conception of perfection excludes both a Calvinist predestination and Luther's stress on the corruption of the will.

Nevertheless many congregations among the forty-odd Methodist Churches with 30,000,000 members—14,400,000 adults—hardly differ from the most liberal parishes of Calvinist origin. Worship has often been replaced by a social gathering, and Eucharistic communion, which Wesley wished very frequent, has become extremely rare. The popular form of Methodism today looks exactly like the popular form of Calvinism in many Presbyterian, Congregational, or Baptist churches. It nonetheless remains favorable ground to religious revivals. Its indifference to doctrine and its emphasis on experience imply a need for occasional reactions. Methodism is one of the most important forces of the Protestant world.

THE SECTS

There is no universally guiding principle for a classification of the sects. Even if we restrict our survey to the most representative, it is clear from the outset that no generalization can be satisfactory. To be near the facts, classification has to be established on tendencies rather than on permanent features. And even so, what seems a prevailing tendency to the outsider may appear utterly different to the man who sees it from within the sectarian experience.

The reader should also make sure that he does not understand "sectarian" in a derogatory sense. Whatever may be thought of the objective value of the sectarian movements, this judgment may not be applied without proviso to the realm of spiritual experience, where the sects find, in final analysis, a more or less adequate justification. A certain insight—the religious implications of which are usually blended with psychological and social resentment—did not find a favorable milieu in the classical Churches. The need was then felt to form a new group essentially limited to those who shared that insight. It matters little that the insight may belong to the realm of piety or that of belief, that it may present itself as a better interpretation of Christianity or as a new gospel: the same need in all these cases ends by forming a sect.

According to the contents of its message or to its prevailing tendencies we may distinguish several groups of sects. We would call them the pietist, the millenarian, and the gnostic types.

As the words would seem to suggest, the essential point of the *pietist sect* is that it separates itself from the world to insure the best conditions of development of "true piety." Thus the Mennonite Brotherhood (Menno Simons, 1496-1561), with some 57,000 members in Europe and 155,000 in America, focuses its life on "absolute love and non violence." Thus the Church of the Brethren (founded in Germany in 1708 and having some 200,000 members in the United States) rejects every creed other than the letter of the New Testament, professions of faith having been experienced somehow as limits imposed from the outside to the spiritual development of Christians. We would also mention here the Society of Friends (Quakers) founded by George Fox in England in 1647 (174,000 members in the world; 115,000 in America alone). It is a community gathered around the "inner light" of the Spirit considered as religiously anterior to Scripture. The Spirit inspires the Friends to activity according to the spiritual needs of the times: at the present day they are mostly philanthropic. Separation from the world is here mainly experienced in worship, the Friends practicing a "free cult" where the community prays in silence and listens to those who have a spiritual message to impart.

The pietist type of sect thus proceeds from a wish to be faithful to the Spirit, which is apparently hindered by the cultural, dogmatic, or cultural structure of the classical Churches.

The *millenarian sect* places the doctrine of the second coming of Christ at the core of Christianity. It results from two converging lines. In the first place, the fundamentalist attitude—to be found also in large sections of the Calvinist Churches in America—interprets the Bible neither according to a doctrinal tradition nor by comparison with its context, but rather according to the strictly literal sense of some Biblical words or verses taken as the key of the whole. Thus all prophetic parts of the Bible are read in the light of Apocalypse 20:4. In the second place, a dissatisfaction with the present state of the world suggests the idea of trying to discover signs that the end of the world is in sight. Hence the conviction that the final judgment is at hand, and sometimes the claim to date it beforehand.

The contemporary form of millenarianism calls itself "adventist" and is divided into a great number of more or less germane sects. Organized in 1845 by the followers of William Miller after the "great disappointment" caused by the failure of the world to end on October 22, 1844— as Miller had announced it—the Adventist Churches total more than 300,000 members in the United States. The most powerful of them is the Church of the Seventh-Day Adventists, so called because, in the words of one of its faithful, "Seventh-Day Adventists have never been able to find a single text in the Bible suggesting that Christ authorized a change of the Sabbath from the seventh to the first day of the week."[3] It had in 1951 some 250,959 members in America and 505,205 in other regions.

Among the millenarian sects we may also list the numerous "Churches of God" that flourish in various parts of the United States. Some of them see their apocalyptic expectation anticipated in the experience of "speaking with other tongues as the Spirit gives utterance," which is "the initial evidence of the baptism of the Holy Ghost."[4] Various other groups, like the Pentecostal Churches, the Assemblies of God, the Church of Christ, the Church of the Foursquare Gospel, etc., also emphasize the coming of the Spirit in a style of worship that follows a revivalistic pattern.

The *gnostic sects* have the common characteristic that they have renounced Christianity and substituted or added a further dogmatic. The Jehovah's Witnesses, the Church of Christ, Scientist, and the Church of Jesus Christ of the Latter-Day Saints (Mormons) represent three varieties of "improvements" on the teaching of Christ. They would have no title to be listed here were they not too often mistaken for genuine Protestant Churches. But there is

[3] Arthur S. Maxwell, in *Look,* March 10, 1953.
[4] Declaration of faith of the Church of God, Cleveland, Tennessee.

nothing common between a Protestant Christian and an initiate of these movements. It is important to distinguish between an imperfect Christianity, like that of the separated Churches and, at a further stage of decay, of the sects, and a non-Christian religion such as may be found in the gnostic sects of our day.

Chapter Three

BASIC DOCTRINES

LUTHER's struggle with the Church originated in a disagreement on the nature of justification. Nowadays, however, the Protestant world in general has removed that problem from the forefront of its concerns. Although one should not unduly generalize, its manifold tendencies are nevertheless truly united by common aspects. The elements of that unity do not always keep the same relationship to one another; yet similar features are to be noticed in both the most conservative and the most radical Reformed communities. Without passing judgment on individual cases, the most essential problems for modern Protestantism seen as a whole may be classified in the following order: the sufficiency of the Bible, the invisible Church, justification and sacraments, optional beliefs, ethics as a personal discovery.

The problem of faith is no other than the question of meeting Christ. In any communion whatsoever, to believe is to have faith in Christ. Differences arise as soon as one tries to define where Christ is encountered (in the Church His mystical Body, according to Catholicism; in Scripture according to the Reformation), under what exterior forms faith is to be affirmed (the objects of belief as listed in the creeds and the various professions of faith), or else what are the results of the act of faith (intrinsic or imputed justification). The encounter with Christ is rightly located at the crossroad of the Christian communions. For the modern world has opened its mind to the notion of "presence." Presence to self and presence to the world constitute the two rival and sometimes contradictory focal points of nonreligious thought. Presence to Christ provides the starting point and the goal of all religious aspirations.

The first affirmation of Protestantism in this juncture is that we are present to Christ only when He Himself is present to us. Christianity is a religion of salvation through grace. Grace is the condescending presence of Christ to the men that He saves. And the proper means adopted by Christ to achieve that presence is the Scripture. Being the personal Word of God, He chose to approach us under the appearance of human words committed to writing in a number of small books for the benefit of men through the centuries. Their sum total is called the Bible, which means *the* Book, beyond which there is nothing to search for because there is nothing beyond. True enough, the first preaching was made by word of mouth, and the Gospels were written down after a few decades of oral tradition. But this is secondary. The main point is, human words then conveyed the message of the New Testament, with the assistance promised by Christ to Peter: "Thou art Rock and on this Rock I will build my Church, and the Gates of Hell shall not prevail against it" (Matt. 16:18). Because the apostles, like Peter, did witness that Jesus was the Christ, the Church is established until the end of time, not on the sand of human opinions, but on the rock of their faith as expressed in Scripture: "Behold, I am with you until the consummation of the world" (Matt. 28:20).

When he looks at Catholicism, a Protestant who is aware of the unique value of the Word of God feels deep sadness. For it seems to him that Catholics do not rest satisfied with the Word of God, that they couple with it, and sometimes even replace it by, another sort of word, human in its origin even though it may come from persons of great holiness or wide knowledge. What Catholicism calls Tradition is understood as the authorized language of centuries of faith. It cannot be mistaken because it is the witness of the Church to which Christ promised assistance. Yet the Protestant mind interprets it as an endeavor to replace the Word of God by what past or present men have thought they grasped of the Gospel. The notion of authoritative Tradition—especially when it is called a source of faith equal to Scripture—repels Protestants. The Reformation prefers the relatively simple formulations of Holy Scripture rather than to entrust its faith to developments that have superseded the primitive simplicity. The commentaries, deductions, assertions, and intellectual adventures forming the Tradition repel Protestants. God has spoken and He has spoken through the Bible. Whatever man may add to it is impious, even when man is faithful.

Especially in its early representatives, the Reformed doctrine nevertheless wants to be infinitely respectful of the Fathers of the Church. Luther and Calvin constantly refer to St. Augustine. But one has to distinguish between an authoritative and an explanatory tradition. It is useful and sometimes necessary to know the thought of the great religious figures of the past. Yet God's assistance to His Church—interpreted by Protestantism—does not guarantee that those men were not mistaken. Any human word added to the Word of God betrays it, simply because it is infinitely beneath it. Neither the sum total of the Fathers nor that of theologians or the Ecumenical Councils, in this view, may claim infallibility. Since the Church is human a total absence of error is an utter impossibility. The Word of God alone is infallible. Man has to read it again and again with humility, constantly to redress what the formulations of faith add to it.

Anglican thought in general does not go so far. It usually acknowledges the normative value of Tradition. However, the separation of the formerly undivided Church into several branches—all of which are, to various degrees, actively or passively guilty of schism—seems to impose on Anglican theologians the saddened conviction that only the early, undivided Tradition has absolute value. Since the eleventh century and especially the sixteenth, no tradition of one particular "church" would preserve, to their eyes, the infallibility that used to be bestowed on the one Tradition of yore. Until the Church becomes again undivided, only Patristic Tradition is considered normative by Anglicanism.

We must finally mention, to make this short survey somehow complete, that two opposite phenomena characterize the sects. For some of them the notion of Scripture tends to recede before the doctrine of the inner light whereby every believer is guided by the Holy Spirit. Thus George Fox once interrupted a sermon with the words: "O no, it is not the Scriptures . . . [but] the Holy Spirit—by which the holy men of God gave forth the Scriptures—whereby opinions, religions and judgments [are] to be tried."[1] Others join to a similar understanding of individual inspiration what American Protestants call fundamentalism, namely, the idea that every word in Scripture may be taken as the foundation of faith, even separated from all context, simply because it expresses a Word of God. Thus one may read in a profession of faith of the Church of God of Cleveland (Tennessee): "We believe, in the verbal inspiration of the Bible, . . . in the baptism with the Holy Ghost subsequent to a clean heart, in speaking with other tongues as the Spirit gives utterance, and that it is the initial evidence of the baptism of the Holy Ghost. . . ."

Inasmuch as the importance of Tradition dwindles, the notion of visible Church is consequently watered down. This parallel plight of two theological doctrines helps us

[1] *Journal,* abridged ed., P. L. Parker, p. 36.

understand the conception of the Church that is advocated
in the Churches of the Reformation. As Luther said it,
"The primary reality which is essentially, fundamentally,
truly the Church we call the spiritual, inner Christendom.
The other, which is a human creation, we call the bodily,
exterior Christendom."[2] This is logical. For if the visible
Church is endowed with no traditional norm for reading
Scripture, she cannot demand absolute obedience from
those who interpret Scripture according to faith. The true,
spiritual, divine Church is then the spiritual union of all
who receive Scripture, read the Word of God in it, and
perceive the message of justification. Calvinists and Lutherans therefore reject the Catholic doctrine of the visible
Church's being a divine institution. The various emphases
in their reading of the Bible, following the different points
of departure that we have mentioned, entail similar stresses
in their views on the Church.

Lutheranism in general is deeply concerned with the
"bodily, exterior" Church. The Church is anterior to the
believer since in her he is born to faith. She is entrusted
with the infinitely delicate role of teacher and counselor.
The faith of the visible Church assists each faithful when
he discovers his Savior, when he reads the message of
justification and is thus introduced into the spiritual
Church. In Calvinism, on the contrary, faith is primary,
and the faith of a community of believers constitutes the
visible Church: "Wherever we see that the Word of God
is purely preached and listened to, and the sacraments
administered according to Christ's institution, we must not
doubt that the Church of God has some existence there."[3]
As for the invisible Church, it comprises all who are predestined to heaven and is known to God only.

Here again the radical ecclesiology of the sects has grown
from Calvinism: the sects themselves hardly differ from

[2] *Treatise on the Papacy,* 1520.
[3] *Institutes,* IV, 1, 9.

some American Churches of Calvinist tradition. The sectarian spirit tends to identify a given community, the sect, with the spiritual Church. This consciousness of belonging to a predestined group underlies, for instance, the following claim of a Seventh-Day Adventist: "Adventists believe that their Church constitutes the nucleus of a twentieth-century Reformation, a world-wide revival of New Testament Christianity."[4]

The sects are far from the humble admission, made both by the Catholic Church and by the Protestant communities of classical pattern, that they form a mixed group where sin and faith coexist, where each member is more sinner than just. The sect on the contrary wants perfection here and now, and its concern for pureness sometimes ends in a naïve sort of perfectionism.

As for the official Anglican conception, it is based on two complementary principles. On the one hand true apostolic succession belongs to the *bene esse* or even the *esse* of the Church. On the other, "the visible Church of Christ is a congregation of faithful men, in which the pure Word of God is preached, and the Sacraments be duly administered according to Christ's ordinance, in all those things that of necessity are requisite to the same" (nineteenth article). The former aspect is Catholic and the latter Calvinist. As understood by Anglican theology, they should normally coincide. Yet every community where one at least is preserved is entitled to be considered part of the Holy Catholic Church spread throughout the world, divided by man's sin in spite of the explicit intention of Jesus Christ. The chasm that Luther introduced between the visible and the invisible has here been transformed into a historical dichotomy between the Church according to Christ's will and the Church as realized by man.

The Catholic conception of the visible Church, which is the efficacious sign, the sacrament, of the invisible, im-

[4] Arthur S. Maxwell, in *Look*, March 10, 1953.

plies a realistic conception of justification and sacramental life. Likewise, the notion of the Church in the theology of the Reformed Churches corresponds either with a more extrinsic view of justification (according to which grace would cover up sins without annihilating them) or with a less realistic conception of the sacraments.

In his fight against the preaching of indulgences, and already in his commentaries on the Psalms, Luther identified justification with the imputation to sinners of the righteousness of Christ: man in himself is not interiorly justified, but in the power of his faith he fully adheres to the saving acts of Christ. Being a sinner, he can paradoxically trust, from the depths of his despair, in the good tidings he reads in the Epistle to the Romans and in Genesis: "Abraham believed God and his faith was imputed to him as righteousness" (Gen. 15:6; Rom. 4:3). Though he knew of the Messiah only by anticipation, Abraham believed; so much the more must we believe today, who, although sinners, have received the message of salvation in Jesus. Thus sinners are justified by grace through faith, without being transformed in their being. When they come to the sacraments (the two sacraments of baptism and the Eucharist, the only ones that are explicitly mentioned in the New Testament), they grasp a token of their salvation in Christ, by association to His death and resurrection in baptism, by reception of His Body and Blood in the Eucharist.

Many sections of the modern Lutheran Churches nevertheless adhere to a Calvinist doctrine on the points in question. Continental Calvinism would explain, as a rule, that sinners are interiorly justified by faith alone (Calvin would have added: according to an eternal decree of predestination). Methodism would think that they are justified by the works of faith. This standpoint is therefore closer to the Catholic Tradition. Yet the sense of the Church is now fading away in the doctrine of the sacramental order. For Calvin the presence of Christ is truly "real" in the Eucharist; but over against the ideas of a presence under the appearances (Catholicism) or in the reality (Lutheranism) of bread and wine, it is only associated to and given with bread and wine. As explained by Calvin, the Body and Blood of Christ become truly present in the soul of Christians who receive the bread and wine with faith in the promise of Christ.

Speaking in general, popular Calvinism today and even popular Lutheranism have in some areas further diluted the thought of Calvin. There is no presence of Christ any more, whether "real physical" or "real spiritual." There is only evocation, remembrance, recalling, or memorial. The sacrament is entirely created by faith, when it is not a mere social rite. This shift of emphasis toward the Protestant left wing has meant for many local congregations the all but complete oblivion of the practice of the Last Supper. This change in doctrine and piety has even reached Methodism, in spite of the explicit intentions of Wesley.

The "lower" sections of the Anglican communion have also been affected by Calvinist and Zwinglian ideas concerning the Eucharist. Yet the understanding of catholicity which is proper to the Anglican Church as a whole has provided support to a full realism as regards justification and the sacraments. Not seldom do we read formulations of those two doctrines that may be accepted as they are by Catholic theology. The typically Anglican stress on the dignity of worship, on cultus as the main work of the Church, on the unanimity of the faithful in the acts of their common prayer, has preserved and even increased the corporate meaning of sacramental life. It is true that at certain periods of its history Calvinist influence threatened to wipe away the "catholic" tendency of the Church of England. Yet a number of Anglican parishes have now developed interesting manifestations of fellowship centered on the sacramental and liturgical life. The social habits of Anglo-

Saxon countries have helped to bring home to many Anglicans the true doctrine of Catholic unanimity in worship, beyond their ambiguous formularies.[5]

Envisaged from the standpoint of their objects, the Lutheran faith bears immediately on salvation through Christ. The Calvinist faith reaches, through an equally selective movement, the Word of God as recorded in Scripture. The Anglican faith in general, though with innumerable variations in practice, believes "what the undivided Church teaches." There is no denial that a general body of doctrine exists, that a number of formularies and confessions deserve to be called Christian and may therefore be considered as the object or the contents of faith from an analytical point of view. The problem consists in establishing a relation between the event of the Incarnation and the progressive unfolding of the contents of the Christian message.

The solution of such a problem is simple. What expresses directly the evangelic message will be required belief. What is connected with this Christian Gospel only through a philosophy or the unhampered flights of pious imagination will be labeled optional belief or even, as the case may be, superstition. Thus Calvinism and Lutheranism agree in totally rejecting the dogmas that have developed inside the Catholic Tradition if they are not explicitly mentioned in the letter of Scripture itself. Anglicanism, on the contrary, with its special interpretation of catholicity, accepts in practice those dogmas as optional beliefs: what only a section of Christendom considers as of faith may be proposed to, not imposed on, the Anglican conscience. Anglicanism thus believes it remains in the Patristic line of thought exemplified in the famous "canon" of St. Vincent of Lérins: "In the Catholic Church one must be very care-

[5] The same remark would apply to some *Hochkirche* sections of Lutheranism.

ful to hold what has been believed everywhere, always and by all."

The continental Reformation thus denies the value of dogmatic development, which provides the very structure of Catholic doctrine on the object of faith and presides over the Catholic interpretation of history. The Church of England, traditionally following its *via media,* holds a mitigated form of it which is counterweighted by its peculiar understanding of the present universality of the Church. Nevertheless, the Churches of the Reformation have not always practiced the same application of their principles. The Reformers, for instance, kept a tender piety toward the Blessed Virgin Mary and faith in her basic privileges (divine Motherhood and Virginity). Luther wrote a fine commentary on the *Magnificat* (1521) and Oecolampadius a small *De laudando in Maria Deum* (1521). Some currents in contemporary Protestantism happily recover this Reformation Mariology. But the great bulk of it has abandoned on that point the faith of the Reformers and dockets "Roman idolatry" on all Marian devotion.

It is thus possible to successive Protestant generations to apply the same principles in contradictory manner. Although this is to be regretted from the standpoint of the Reformation itself, which wanted to be equally evangelical in all things, there is no ground to see in it catastrophic "variations" (to use Bossuet's expression). It is a matter of divergences in questions deemed unessential.

Similar differences are to be noticed as regards ethics. The general principle of the Reformed Churches is clear: there is no "natural" ethics, since the nature of man has been vitiated by sin. There is no "revealed" ethics either, since Revelation is not the proclamation of a "law" but the undeserved gift of salvation in Christ. There is only a gracious call toward God for all that have been made cognizant of the good tidings of justification by faith. "Love and do what you will," St. Augustine said: for the lover will discover in the intuitions of love what pleases his beloved. The ethics of the Reformation are no other than the personal unselfish discovery of what is right to the eyes of God. Since we deal with Christians, men who have been justified by faith, what looks to the outsider like individual initiative or effort toward righteousness is in reality the work of the Holy Spirit. What seems chaos or indifference to the stranger is no other than respect for the patience of God, who leads men neither to the same goal nor along the same path. When a particular Church provides practical rules of behavior, these represent no more than an average judgment on the minimum rectitude implied in a sincere profession of Christian faith; but like everything human, this appreciation may vary. Protestantism accordingly has no constant doctrine on the indissolubility of marriage. Yet its tolerance of divorce—which is entirely banned in some Churches—does not drive away the fact that it still upholds indissoluble matrimony as the Christian ideal. Too many people are persuaded that Protestantism has no ethics; this impression runs foul of Protestant doctrine and of the everyday experience of a fervent Protestant life.

It is nevertheless quite true that the practice of the various Reformed communities swings to and fro between the extremes of puritanism and of moral laxity. The former is often associated with the sects, where it constitutes a safeguard from the world. It replaces moral aspiration with social conformity inside of a given group. The latter is a permanent danger for the Churches born of the Reformation: it forgets moral aspiration and slips down the way of our largely immoral secular societies.

This rapid glance at the basic religious thought of the Reformation points to one obvious fact: the Reformation is not—as too many believe who are not conversant with its doctrine and mentality—a denial of Christianity; it is a biased interpretation of the faith. When we lump together Protestant and unbeliever, we spirit away the problem of Protestantism; but suppression is never a solution. By this we then adopt a standpoint from which we cannot see that there is a problem. And this leads to a disastrous consequence for the catholicity of our thought. The Catholic who is aware of the profound nature of his faith must be open to all human dramas. The drama of Protestantism is that of the 200,000,000 Christians—or approximately so—who adhere to the theology of the Reformation. This raises a serious religious problem. For those millions of Christians undergo an actual, though slanted, experience of faith of which we do not partake and which is nonetheless real.

At this point in our inquiry, the problem seems therefore to consist in acquiring a sufficient acquaintance with the theology of the Reformation by discerning its human and Christian undertones without renouncing an iota of the spiritual, intellectual, and moral implications of the Catholic faith.

Chapter Four

ANTI-ROMAN PREJUDICES

PROTESTANTS who are acquainted with the history of their Churches know what adjectives Luther used and misused when he spoke of the Pope, and those who are without culture have also inherited a long past of insults and prejudices. No objective account of contemporary Protestantism, even when it tries to understand the religious substance of the Reformation, can overlook this aspect of things. Unfortunately both Catholics and non-Catholics sin against each other through mutual ignorance and reciprocal prejudices. It does seem, however, that nowadays the Protestant side has outrun the other in piling up hasty judgments, mistaken ideas, and ridiculous legends. This is a heavy heritage from past centuries. As successive generations hand it along, they also increase its load year after year.

The anti-Catholic, or, to be more exact, the anti-Roman, prejudice has such an influence on the formation of the Protestant conscience that one must speak of it, in order precisely to judge it dispassionately and correct it when occasion arises. It goes without saying, however, that to speak of an anti-Roman complexus is not tantamount to making every non-Catholic a victim to it. A number of Christians in all denominations are not tainted with it.

The reader will also kindly recall what good we have had to say about the Reformers and their spiritual children. To analyze defects in the Protestant mentality does not mean that we try to belittle the Protestant position. It means that we wish to purify the imperfections that the Reformation fostered.

When his interpretation of the faith was rejected by the Papacy, Luther was brought to identify the Pope and Antichrist. This identification is still maintained by the most conservative kind of Lutheranism. Although many Lutherans would smile it away, as though it were an innocent prank or an overforceful but understandable excess of language, the following lines may be read in a doctrinal statement from the Missouri Synod:

> As to the Antichrist we teach that the prophecies of the Holy Scriptures concerning the Antichrist have been fulfilled in the Pope of Rome and his dominion. All the features of the Antichrist as drawn in these prophecies, including the most abominable and horrible ones, for example, that the Antichrist "as God sitteth in the Temple of God"; that he anathematizes the very heart of the Gospel of Christ, that is, the doctrine of the forgiveness of sins by grace alone, for Christ's sake alone, through faith alone, without any merit or worthiness in man; that he recognizes only those as members of the Christian Church who bow to his authority; and that, like a deluge, he had inundated the whole Church with his antichristian doctrines till God revealed him through the Reformation,—these very features are the outstanding characteristics of the Papacy. Hence we subscribe to the statement of our Confessions that the Pope is the very Antichrist.[1]

According to the 1953 Convention of the Missouri Synod, held at Houston, Texas, this identification of the Pope with Antichrist is not held as a doctrine of faith necessary

[1] *Brief Statement of the Doctrinal Position of the Missouri Synod,* 1931.

to salvation but as a judgment passed on historical facts.

At the most friendly extreme of the many shades of anti-Romanism let us take stock of a passage in the report on the unity of the Church submitted to the Lambeth Conference of 1948: "We are frankly puzzled by the apparent contradiction between the repeated general invitations to coöperation which the Pope himself has issued and the attitude of many Roman Catholics in particular countries when it comes to definite programmes. . . ." One may sense here a great respect for the modern Papacy as well as a regret that some Catholics feel they have to be, as the saying goes, "more Catholic than the Pope." The highest prelate of the Anglican communion, Dr. Geoffrey Fisher, has, however, not yet outgrown a recurrent form of anti-Romanism. He thought it wise to declare to the Convocation of Canterbury on October 1, 1953, referring to the Roman Catholic Church: "It must be recognised that, in past and present history, a Church claiming more than its due may try to advance the kingdom of God by the employment of political force, and by the denial of just liberties. The Roman Catholic Church has not yet learned the lesson that toleration as between Christian bodies, while by no means the last word as to their proper relations, is the essential word to those who would follow the teaching of our Lord."[2] A pamphlet colorfully called *Infallible Fallacies,* which the English Archbishop then advertised as an effective instrument to answer back "Roman propagandists," contains an unfortunate hodgepodge of mistakes, omissions, and downright libel.

As a rule, however, when Anglicans criticize the Catholic Church, they do it more moderately, denouncing, rather than the Church in general or the Papacy, the behavior of Catholics themselves or what non-Catholics call "Rome," that is, the administrative apparatus which surrounds the primacy of the Supreme Pontiff, and which has been made

[2] *Church Times,* October 16, 1953.

all but indispensable by the growing intricacies of modern life.

A constant point of friction between Catholics and Protestants is provided by the fact that the same realities are differently interpreted. The former see the historical and therefore accidental development of a system of government expressing for our time the invariable structure of the Church. The latter claim to discern an introduction of political conceptions in the government of the Church: whence the idea, which is regularly fanned by the press of a certain kind of Protestantism, that every Roman decision proceeds from a vast political plan covering all the world. Into the encyclicals, where Catholics hear the motherly voice of the Church warning them against dangers and exaggerations, Protestants are tempted to read a system of intellectual and spiritual dictatorship opposing the course of history and the development of culture. When a precision is added to a point of doctrine or discipline, as for instance with the recent decrees on the form of the sacrament of Order or the Eucharistic fast, the Catholic is happy to find safe, though slow, adaptations, while others trace the curve of the "variations" of the Catholic Church. Having adequate information, Catholics make the required distinctions between Canon Law and doctrine, between dogma and theology, between infallible definitions and fatherly admonitions or theological and historical exposés, between an authentic interpretation of Scripture and its liturgical or allegorical use; while non-Catholics, untrained to decipher the style of pontifical texts, fall into fatal misreadings.

One can hardly exaggerate the responsibility of Catholics themselves in this vast misinterpretation of the Roman interventions in the life of the Church. Too many ignorant journalists misrepresent facts and documents; too many equally ignorant priests misunderstand them and explain them out of their true sense; too many textbooks, catechisms, pamphlets, articles, and posters streamline them out of recognition; too many apologetical or theological essays expound the doctrine so one-sidedly that plenty of good will and discernment are needed to understand it in all its catholicity. Protestants cannot take the blame when Catholics themselves overlook or forget the distinctions, emphases, and contexts apart from which any doctrine will be misstated. An oversimplified presentation of facts makes it unavoidable that authority, seen from the outside, looks like tyranny. Obedience then seems to be servile. Caution is mistaken for petrification, and courage for arrogance.

Through no mere coincidence, the most rampant anti-Catholicism is to be met in regions where, or at times when, the behavior of Catholics themselves has something strait-laced, unbending, and self-conceited about it. This excessive rigidity is not native to Catholicism as such. Yet it gives the impression that some Catholics conceive their faith as a kind of fanaticism on the warpath. Thus the hysterical anti-Papism of John Kensit and his followers used to be an English phenomenon. The militant anti-Catholicism of Paul Blanshard has more recently been an American phenomenon. American Catholics have always been noted for their devoted Eucharistic and Marian piety and their tender reverence for the person of the Supreme Pontiff. Like all American groups, they also suffer from a certain dearth of historical and theological culture. And this in turn provides occasions to recurrent outbursts of anti-Romanism, when many distinguished (and other) Protestants chronically border on the grotesque by raising a phony war cry about the "political aims of the Vatican."[3]

We now come to more theological questions. One fact strikes all Catholics who are familiar with Protestant theology: even the most enlightened and best informed Prot-

[3] This mutual conditioning of two attitudes has a clear precedent in the reciprocal influence of the Reformation and the Counter Reformation. In the context of the Latin countries the correlation of clericalism and anticlericalism provides an instance of a similar pattern of reactions.

estant thinkers fall into gross and even childish errors when they report Catholic doctrine.

I find in the works of an eminent theologian the following criticisms of Catholic positions. The Catholic Church is identified with religious heteronomy; it is static and formalistic; it deforms Christianity in an overintellectualistic direction; it represents a return to the magic and demonic phase of the development of mankind; it hides the Biblical message under a supernatural ontology; it teaches moral legalism; its sacramental theology destroys the religious depth of Christianity; it builds up an ethical rationalization of the Spirit; it is based on the historical fallacy of episcopal succession; it entails fanaticism; it is theologically stagnant.

It is always a refreshing experience to see oneself through the glasses of another. Yet there is no doubt that in the present case the glasses are out of focus. For as a whole these reproaches rest on basically false interpretations of Catholicism, probably because they come from someone who has no personal experience of what he writes about. Now every criticism made from the outside always lacks the immediately existential touch without which any profound religious insight remains hopelessly beyond reach. Moreover, some of the items listed illegitimately ascribe to the Church as such what pertains to some of her members, or to her essence what applies to accidents of her history. It would be tiresome to take up those points one by one. Yet one of them at least betrays most clearly the anti-Roman prejudice. The Church, we are told, represents a return to the magic and demonic phase of the development of mankind. If we closely examine this, it refers to the Catholic conception of sacramental causality: a sacrament, according to Catholic theology, works, not *ex opere operantis,* but *ex opere operato.*

I have long been nonplused by the fact that many Protestants consider the sacraments of the Catholic Church as magical devices, whereas the same sacraments given in the

Orthodox Churches look to them like interesting elements of a venerable, if overrated, world outlook. I now believe I have found why the same sacraments are thus differently judged according as they are given by a Catholic or by an Orthodox priest. Reading and listening to the theologian I have mentioned, I have noticed that he understands *non ex opere operantis* as meaning "independently of the dispositions of faith of the man who receives the sacrament." Now in Catholic doctrine it means "independently of the holiness of the man who confers the sacrament." We face here a mere Latin misreading transmitted by Protestant theologians from professor to student. Since, on the other hand, Orthodox theology does not use the Latin expression —simply because Latin is not its customary language—its doctrine is respected, while the same doctrine in its Latin formula is labeled "magical."

This nearly pure case of anti-Roman prejudice may be taken as a symbol of what immense misunderstanding has to be cleared up on many points where Protestant theology has forgotten its Catholic starting point. Misunderstanding, no need to add, works both ways; and this renders all the more difficult the hard though pressing task of untying so many intertwined threads.

Chapter Five

SEARCHING FOR UNITY

MODERN ecumenism is a common search after Christian unity by Churches that do not know or that misunderstand the Catholic unity of the Church of Rome and its historical continuity with the Church of the Middle Ages, the Fathers, and the Apostles. There is only one "great Church," as the Fathers said: it is to be known from its communion with the successor of Peter, the Bishop of Rome. The ecumenical movement, on the contrary, starts from the existence of separated Christian communions and it tries to go forward to a unity which is not considered as already achieved or given. From the Catholic point of view, the ecumenical movement is therefore a paradox. Yet however we may judge it, we have to envisage and study it objectively. It is a search after a universal visible unity by Christians who stand outside visible membership in the Catholic Church.

The ecumenical movement must be assessed from the level of Christian witness and experience: in reference to the great realities of Christian life and doctrine, it purports to incite each one to criticize his own behavior toward Christians of other Churches. It is therefore, first and foremost, spiritual. Yet it implies a theology that we will have to outline. It is also a historical phenomenon, the main lines of whose development we will now sketch.

In the shape it has adopted in our day, the ecumenical movement is relatively recent. One has to go far back in the history of the Protestant Churches, however, to find its remote origins. Christian unity had pioneers in the Protestant world soon after the Reformation had provoked a multiplication of denominations. Thus the English Puritan Richard Baxter, in the seventeenth century, proposed the following course: "To come as near together as we can possibly in our principles; and when we cannot, yet to unite as far as may be in our practise, though on different principles; and where that cannot be, yet to agree on the most loving, peaceable course in this way of carrying on our different practices."[1] A desire for visible unity was clear in the foundation of a number of Biblical societies. The Religious Tract Society of 1799 and the British and Foreign Bible Society of 1804 both had an interdenominational basis. Likewise, the London Missionary Society of 1794 adopted as its fundamental principle: "Our desire is not to send Presbyterianism, Independency, Episcopacy, or any other form of Church Order and Government (about which there may be differences of opinion among serious Persons) but the glorious Gospel of the Blessed God to the Heathen."[2]

The idea of a possible union between Christians of various persuasions was destined to make headway most quickly in missionary circles. A Baptist preacher, William Carey, meeting an Anglican missionary, Henry Martyn, at Serampore, India, in 1806, suggested that delegates from all missions should meet once every ten years at the Cape of Good Hope (made into a symbol of hope in Christian unity). Being somewhat overoptimistic, Carey envisaged the first convention for 1810. The idea spread little by little during the nineteenth century. In 1854 missionary assemblies were or-

---

[1] Dedication of his *Saints' Everlasting Rest*, in *Works*, Vol. XXIII, p. 8.
[2] Quoted in Richard Lovett, *History of the London Missionary Society*, Vol. I, pp. 49-50.

ganized by Dr. Alexander Duff in Great Britain and the United States. A similar meeting was held at Liverpool in 1860. In 1878 thirty-four missionary societies sent delegates to London, and one hundred and twenty did the same in 1888. The following meeting, which took place in New York in 1900, called itself "ecumenical." The most important conference met at Edinburgh in 1910; to a great extent the modern ecumenical movement dates back to this Edinburgh Conference.

The ecumenical idea was also developed in the youth movements. The famous association of Protestant youths, YMCA, had been founded in 1878 on an international and interdenominational basis; the corresponding girls' movement followed in 1894. The next year, 1895, one of the great pioneers of ecumenism, the American John Mott, took a decisive step when he established the World Student Christian Federation, made up of Protestants from all countries and traditions. The special interest of youths in the missions resulted in a joint effort with the missionary societies for the preparation of the Edinburgh Conference of 1910.

The Archbishop of Canterbury, William Temple, declared once that the Edinburgh Conference had been "the greatest event in the life of the Church for a whole generation." It created a permanent commission, the International Missionary Council (plenary sessions at Jerusalem in 1928, at Tambaram near Madras in 1938, at Whitby, Canada, in 1947). Moreover, the *Faith and Order* movement, which organized one of the first ecumenical assemblies properly so called, also derived from the Edinburgh Conference.

While he was touring the United States on his way back from Edinburgh, Charles Brent, Episcopalian Bishop of the Philippines, advocated a similar meeting that would deal with doctrinal questions. Following this hint, the Protestant Episcopal Church of the United States adopted a resolution at its Cincinnati convention of October, 1910, to the effect that a committee should be formed, which would take "steps to bring about a conference for the consideration of questions touching *Faith and Order* and that all Christian communions throughout the world which confess our Lord Jesus Christ as God and Savior be asked to meet with us in arranging and conducting such a conference." This marked the beginning of the *Faith and Order* movement. Thanks to the efforts of an American, Robert H. Gardiner, the proposed meeting was held at Lausanne in 1927, with 400 delegates coming from 108 Churches, most of them Protestant. The Conference agreed on a formula of faith considered as a minimum membership requirement. This is the most significant passage: "Notwithstanding the differences in doctrine among us, we are united in a common Christian faith, with is proclaimed in the Holy Scriptures, and is witnessed to and safeguarded in the Ecumenical Creed, commonly called the Nicene, and in the Apostles' Creed, which faith is continuously confirmed in the spiritual experience of the Church of Christ."[3]

The doctrinal basis accepted by the delegates who joined the movement was the following. On the one hand Scripture, being the Word of God, is a sufficient norm of faith, the problem of its interpretation being left to the responsibility of each denomination. On the other, the creed of the Council of Nicea is held to be faithful to Scripture and useful to the protection of scriptural doctrine. By thus affirming that a true unity of faith rests on experiences of Christianity that are deemed to converge or to be of equal value, *Faith and Order* assumed from the outset that the main problem was solved: various Churches with divergent and sometimes contradictory beliefs are supposed to be united in faith in spite of their disagreements. The conclusions of the Lausanne Conference entailed therefore the more or less "modernist" idea that the formulations of faith

[3] *Proceedings*, p. 466.

are subordinate to experience and draw their value only from it.

A second assembly was held at Edinburgh in 1937 and decided, among other things, to try and form a *World Council of Churches,* the members of which would be not, as hitherto, qualified individuals but the Churches as such.

While *Faith and Order* was developing, a parallel movement, with a view to achieving practical co-operation on the social level, was also in formation. Here the desire for doctrinal unity was replaced by the wish for a common attitude in the equivocal conflict between Christianity and the world.

A World Alliance for Promoting International Friendship through the Churches had been founded at Constance on August 1, 1914. At the meeting of the Alliance that followed World War I—The Hague, 1919—the Lutheran Archbishop of Upsala, Nathan Söderblom, proposed that a universal Christian meeting should be held that would study the *Life and Work* of Christians.

The first assembly of *Life and Work* was convened at Stockholm in 1925. Its aim is well expressed in the following text:

We believe that there is a longing on the part, not merely of the trusted servants of the Church, but of all followers of our Lord and Master, to see Christendom so far united as to be able to work together in applying the principles taught by Him to the problems which confront us both in national and international life. . . . The common purpose of our Conference therefore will be to discover lines along which we may all unite in endeavoring to meet this grave responsibility. In our deliberations we do not propose to deal with matters of Faith and Order, although we are not unmindful of their importance. Our prayer and hope is that through this Conference a new impetus will be given to the various movements and strivings for reunion, but the world's need is so urgent and the demand for common action on the part of all Christians so insistent at this juncture, that we cannot afford to await the fulfilment of that great hope of a reunited Christendom before putting our hearts and our hands into a united effort that God's will may be done on earth as it is in heaven.[4]

The second assembly met at Oxford in 1937. As was done at Edinburgh that same year, the assembly decided to constitute a *World Council of Churches*. The two movements were thus going to amalgamate.

The first step undertaken was the formation of a provisional committee with William Temple, then Archbishop of York, as its chairman. On account of World War II the first achievements were long delayed but men in the meanwhile devoted more reflection to the purpose of the projected Council.

The first assembly of the *World Council of Churches* met at Amsterdam in 1948. Composed of 351 delegates from 147 Churches and 44 countries, the meeting was mainly concerned with the organization of the Council. It also studied a doctrinal topic that had been prepared over several years. Under the general title of "Man's Disorder and God's Design," four sections were devoted to "The Universal Church in God's Design," "The Church's Witness to God's Design," "The Church and the Disorder of Society," "The Church and the International Disorder." This method, which applies a central theme to modern problems, seems to be really efficient in trying to reach a common awareness of the relevance of the Gospel to the modern world. This does not mean, naturally, that Amsterdam smoothed out divergences. Far from it. Yet its most important achievement resides in the will to "stay together" in spite of wide rifts. The message adopted by the assembly proclaimed: "We are one in acknowledging Christ as our God and Savior. We are divided from one another not only in matters of faith, order and tradition, but also by pride of nation, class and race. But Christ has made us His own and He is not divided. In seeking Him we find one another. Here at Am-

[4] *Official Report*, p. 18.

sterdam we have committed ourselves afresh to Him and have covenanted with one another in constituting this *World Council of Churches*. We intend to stay together. . . ." This intention to continue striving after unity is the most noteworthy contribution of Amsterdam.

The meeting of *Faith and Order* at Lund, Sweden, in 1952 has also to be mentioned. *Life and Work,* having merged into the Council, no longer exists. *Faith and Order,* on the contrary, lives on as a commission inside the Council. Lund was the first world-wide gathering of this commission since the formation of the Council, and the third from the start of the *Faith and Order* movement. This meeting was all the more important as the doctrinal basis of *Faith and Order* had in fact been adopted by the Council itself. The works of this commission are accordingly due to wield an extensive influence throughout the Protestant world. The 226 delegates at Lund studied the nature of the Church, the forms of worship, and the question of intercommunion between Churches. The message adopted insisted particularly that the Churches ought to take most seriously their duty of unity:

We have seen clearly that we can make no real advance towards unity if we only compare our several conceptions of the nature of the Church and the traditions in which they are embodied. . . . We have now reached a crucial point in our ecumenical discussions. As we have come to know one another better our eyes have been opened to the depth and pain of our separations and also to our fundamental unity. The measure of unity which it has been given to the Churches to experience together must now find clearer manifestation. A faith in the one Church of Christ which is not implemented by *acts* of obedience is dead. There are truths about the nature of God and His Church which will remain for ever closed to us unless we act together in obedience to the unity which is already ours. . . .

This call has now to be heard in the denominations. For the *World Council,* as well as its commission on *Faith and*

Order, will betray its purpose if it proves to be no more than a study circle of delegates while the rank and file do not include their conclusions in the warp and woof of their daily life.

The second major assembly of the *World Council of Churches* gathered at Evanston, Illinois, in August, 1954, with 502 delegates from 179 Churches in 54 countries, and a grand total of 1298 official participants. The delegates devoted their time to the study of a main theme, "Christ, the Hope of the World," and six subordinate topics dealing with "our oneness in Christ and our disunity as Churches" (*Faith and Order* commission), evangelism, social questions, international affairs, intergroup relations, and the witness of the laity. The message of the assembly was a word of hope for man in the sore straits where modern society seems to have landed itself. The end of the report on "oneness and disunity" appropriately voices the delegates' reaffirmed willingness to "stay together" and their further wish to "grow together":

Rejoicing in the grace which has been bestowed upon us in His various gifts even in our sin and separateness, we here set our hope in our one Lord Jesus Christ, who comes to take control over our divided and broken estate and to heal it by His grace and power. At Amsterdam we said that we intend to stay together. He has kept us together. He has shown Himself again as our Hope. Emboldened by this Hope, we dedicate ourselves to God anew, that He may enable us to grow together.

More than the preceding meetings, the Evanston Assembly threw light on the paradoxical nature of the *World Council,* which is a fellowship of Churches inside of which denominational traditions and loyalties have been hardened by mutual contact. Far from becoming a smooth-running apparatus tending to progressive unification, it is developing into a sharp instrument of self-criticism among the Protestant Churches.

However this may be, the *World Council* cannot now be lightly dismissed by Catholics. Its doctrinal implications will be outlined in the next chapter. Before we come to them, however, we ought to examine a point of history: What attitude has the *World Council* adopted toward the only Christian body of international significance that has not joined its fellowship in any way, the Roman Catholic Church?

At the beginning of the movement, the organizers of *Faith and Order* and *Life and Work* tried to obtain the participation of Catholics. While the Conference of Stockholm was being prepared, Dr. Henry A. Atkinson, the Secretary General of *Life and Work,* visited Rome personally, and the Archbishop of Upsala renewed this invitation in writing. Both met with a courteous refusal. No further invitation was extended for the Oxford Conference.

The efforts of *Faith and Order* were more numerous and steady. Between November 2, 1914, and April 7, 1915, there took place an exchange of letters between Robert H. Gardiner and Cardinal Gasparri, then Secretary of State at the Vatican.[5] In May, 1919, a formal invitation was sent to Pope Benedict XV. In the following summer the Anglican Bishops of Chicago, Southern Ohio, and Fond du Lac, the Revs. E. L. Parsons and B. Talbot, and Mr. R. W. Brown went to Rome and interviewed Msgr. Ceretti, Cardinal Gasparri, and Benedict XV himself. The delegates were given the impression that the Holy Father took a great personal interest in the venture although he was firmly decided not to join it. In May, 1921, the Archbishop of Canterbury forwarded to the Pope, through the Secretary of State, the text of the "Lambeth Quadrilateral," a resolution passed at the 1920 Lambeth Conference on the requirements of Christian unity according to the Anglican tradition. Finally, in the summer of 1926, Bishop Brent of the Philip-

[5] Text published in Max Pribilla, *Um kirchliche Einheit,* pp. 314-318.

pines called on Pius XI. During all that time the decision
not to take part in "ecumenical" organizations was repeat-
edly made clear. It was finally explained in the encyclical
letter *Mortalium Animos* (January 6, 1928): in the light of
the experiences of Stockholm and Lausanne, the Protestant
movement toward unity was pronounced to be "subversive
of the foundations of the Catholic faith."[6]

In spite of this unequivocal stand, the Archbishop of
York, William Temple, sounded the ground again in view
of the Edinburgh Conference. On September 11, 1936, he
wrote to the Catholic Archbishop of St. Andrews and Edinburgh to the effect that the previous invitations were still
standing, and he left it to the Catholic Archbishop whether
or not the Holy See should be informed of this. The Archbishop's answer arrived in February, 1937, after a second
letter had urged the matter again; he had decided to leave
the question aside. During the assembly, however, he sent
to the delegates a courteous letter that was read in plenary
session.

The formation of the *World Council of Churches* occa-
sioned further approaches. In February, 1939, William
Temple informed the Secretary of State of the projected
foundation. Though he formulated no precise invitation,
he added: "We hope that it may be permissible to exchange
information with agencies of the Church of Rome on matters of common interest and that we should have the help
from time to time of unofficial consultation with Roman
Catholic theologians and scholars." In April, 1947, the
Provisional Committee decided to invite some Catholic
theologians as unofficial observers at Amsterdam. Early in
1948 the number of these was brought down to a dozen,
after many letters asking for an invitation had been received
from Catholics, a number of whom mentioned that they
had secured their Ordinary's approval before writing. In
April, 1948, it was made known to the committee that Car-

[6] Cf. Chapter 8 for the exact meaning of this expression.

dinal de Jong, Archbishop of Utrecht, wished to be consulted for each case, and this information was duly forwarded to the theologians who had been invited. On June 5 a public *Monitum* from the Holy Office recalled that participation of Catholics in non-Catholic religious gatherings needed the previous assent of the Holy See, and that same month Cardinal de Jong was informed that no permission would be granted for the Amsterdam Assembly.[7]

Before the Lund Conference on *Faith and Order* in 1952, Yngve Brilioth, Lutheran Archbishop of Upsala, held an interview with the Vicar Apostolic in Sweden. As a result of this, four Catholic priests were officially designated by the Vicar Apostolic and were publicly received at the assembly as "accredited visitors."

No visitors or observers were sent to the Evanston Conference.

[7] On these details, cf. a memorandum by H. S. Leiper, *Relations Between the Ecumenical Movement and the Vatican in the Twentieth Century.*

Chapter Six

⇢⇢≫≪⇠⇠

THEOLOGY OF ECUMENISM

THE ECUMENICAL movement has to be judged, in ultimate analysis, in accordance with the principles of Catholic theology, while account must be taken of its doctrinal undertones, which themselves originate in the theology of the various Reformed Churches. In our outline of these doctrinal implications, however, we shall confine ourself to the doctrine which is now at the forefront of the ecumenical movement. For the formation of the *World Council of Churches* corresponds to a growing precision of thought in ecumenical circles, whereas formerly divergences were too prominent to permit formation of a common doctrine.

The basic conception of Protestant ecumenism is well illustrated by the following lines written in 1937 by one of the great minds of the movement, Hendrick Kraemer, formerly professor at the University of Leyden and the first director of the Ecumenical Institute of Bossey, Switzerland:

Religion and Church in the essentially Christian sense of the words are no affirmations or apprehensions of absolute values, but express an act of trust and self-committal to the God and Father of Our Lord Jesus Christ. The Church has in God its origin and its center. . . . The Church, however, as the fellowship of those who believe in Christ and love and worship Him, ought never to

75

forget that this fellowship transcends all mundane relations by its loyalty to its Head and Lord. . . . The empirical Church has to confront itself constantly with this mystery of its divinely-willed fellowship, and be cleansed and inspired by it in order to realize a kind of fellowship in the world that has its roots in eternity and thereby manifests a deeper quality than any other form of fellowship can.[1]

The underlying assumptions of Protestant ecumenism may be summed up as follows: Let us imagine three levels of reality, A, B, and C, of which A is the highest, C the lowest, and B intermediary. Protestant thinking tends to conceive of the Church as simultaneously existing on the three levels, with differences of behavior going with the special nature of those planes of existence.

At the highest level, A, the Church is such as God wills it: it is the ideal, the type, which the Church of the earth has to imitate. Yet it is not only an ideal, for God's thought is creative, in the absolute sense of this term. The faithful—that is, not the members of one denomination or another, but all who believe in Christ—are therefore truly one in God. Yet—and this is the crux of the matter—their daily life does not unfold itself on that level and accordingly it is only at privileged moments, when faith raises them above the day-by-day texture of existence, that they are conscious of that unity in God. This mysterious hidden union constitutes the Church of what we have called level A. Everything else has to be judged by reference to it. And since the spiritual structure of this invisible Church cannot be known apart from reading Holy Scripture where God Himself speaks, the final norm that will judge levels B and C is no other than Holy Writ, without the additions of the various Christian traditions, however much or little these ought to be respected.

The inferior level, C, takes us such as we are in everyday experience. Instead of being joined together as at level A,

[1] *The Christian Message in a Non-Christian World,* pp. 417-418.

Christians then live side by side, in Churches that ignore each other and have at times taken up arms one against the other. Even outside of these religious wars they have overlooked the primacy of brotherly love and have exchanged insults. This rivalry and strife is also to be found among individuals. In the Protestant view of things, the visible Church—that is, the sum total of believers—does not constitute on earth a true likeness of what the Church is in God. There is a discontinuity between levels A and C.

We now come to the medium level, B. Let us suppose that, while we still linger on level C, where distinct and often hostile traditions vie with each other in a sometimes unholy competition, we nevertheless try to transform the Church on earth, divided against itself, into a closer likeness of the Church in heaven. Inasmuch as, with God's grace, this is little by little being achieved, we are raised to an intermediary level, B. Here we still deal with this earth and the empirical Church where Christians are separated and their spiritual life is doomed to imperfection. Though condemned never to reach near to its heavenly pattern, this empirical Church now endeavors to be reformed by the power of the Holy Spirit to a better resemblance of the heavenly Church. The intention of Christians makes them somehow live on level A. Yet the conditions of human existence thwart every effort and, necessarily remaining at the inferior level, the faithful achieve but imperfect and partial reforms. The outcome is the Church of level B. It is still a Church of sin and division; but it is aware of the sinfulness of its existence and tries to transcend itself, not through any merit earned by its own acts and techniques, but through utter fidelity to the Word of God.

This basic conception of Protestant ecumenism, which is germane to many a theological attitude in the Churches of the Reformation, calls for an important remark. The notion of the Church that it entails is radically *equivocal,* which means that one expression, "Church," is applied to heterogeneous levels, at each of which it does not cover the same things. It even covers essentially different elements. A break separates levels A and C. And level B, accordingly, which joins characteristics of both, attempts the impossible by trying to unite contradictories. This conception is therefore entirely different from the Catholic doctrine of the Church. In this doctrine there is an *analogy* between the mystical Body of Christ (level A) and the Catholic Church (level B). Analogy means that relations between the divine and the human are the same in both, though they are, in B, expressed and embodied in externals that belong to this world and are therefore incorporated in sociological and institutional structures. As for level C, Catholic theology does not recognize the Church in it: it is the level of human sin, not of the Church as such.

Between Catholicism and ecumenical Protestantism we must therefore register that there is, from this standpoint, an unbridgeable gap, an out-and-out difference. They live in spiritual universes that are not compatible.

From the vantage point we have now reached, we may perceive some of the difficulties that Protestant ecumenism runs into. It is obvious that a world-wide search for unity, jointly made by men who come from all spiritual horizons, cannot be successful overnight, even when all the horizons in question are located within Protestantism. Many obstacles have to be surmounted.

The most basic drawback comes from the divergences that separate the various Protestant traditions. The organizers of the *World Council* tried from the outset to limit those divergences within relatively narrow bounds. Hence they imposed a minimum profession of faith: all member churches of the Council "accept Jesus Christ as God and Savior." Once this basis is assured, however, many differences remain, not only as regards a number of points of detail, but even in respect of the nature of salvation itself.

Thus among the Churches of the World Council the Anglican communion—whose "High-Church" section comes near
to Roman Catholicism on some points—rubs shoulders
with the free Churches, in parts of which salvation in Christ
becomes an emotional experience as in the most radical
sects. The question is, therefore: How can those doctrinal
oppositions be transcended? If we now look at the problem
from farther away and remember that some Orthodox
Churches are represented in the Council, it looks as though
there were a deep abyss between a Catholic-minded and
even a Catholic tradition and the extreme forms of Protestantism. One may perhaps say that a union of opposites
is being attempted, hardly easier than a squaring of a circle.

The following remarks, where Hendrick Kraemer assesses
the situation of Christianity facing pagan religions, may be
applied here:

It ought never to be forgotten in the treatment of religious
subjects—but it constantly is—that religion is the vast and desperate effort of mankind to get somehow an apprehension of the
totality of existence, and therefore every religion is an indivisible,
and not to be divided, unity of existential apprehension. It is not
a series of tenets, dogmas, prescriptions, institutions, practices,
that can be taken one by one as independent items of religious
life, conception or organisation, and that can arbitrarily be compared with, and somehow related to, and grafted upon, the similar
item of another religion. Every religion is a living, indivisible
unity. Every part of it—a dogma, a rite, a myth, an institution, a
cult—is so vitally related to the whole that it can never be understood in its real function, significance and tendency, as these occur
in the reality of life, without keeping constantly in mind the vast
and living unity of existential apprehension in which this part
moves and has its being.[2]

To leave one religion for another, one has entirely to give
up an intellectual and spiritual universe of life. Now, to a
lesser extent, and with important provisos, the same holds

[2] Ibid., p. 135.

true of the Protestant traditions. There is a world of difference between the universe of Anglicanism—with its awareness of the mystery of common worship, its concern for liturgy and adoration—and, for instance, the Calvinist world, with its emphasis on each man's personal vocation and the earnestness with which one must perceive and accept it by becoming conversant with the inner testimony of the Holy Spirit to those who read the Bible with faith. The experience of salvation and of life in Christ has now another direction; and centuries of reflection, prayer, Bible reading, common discoveries and setbacks, sufferings and hopes, persecutions and victories, have provided it with frameworks that cannot be interchanged.

In practice, Protestant ecumenism has tried two ways of overcoming this dilemma.

One of them may be illustrated by the local union of Churches in South India. In 1947, after negotiations that were started in 1919, the Churches of South India—the Catholic Church and the Syro-Malabar Church excepted—agreed to amalgamate on the basis of the following principles:

1. Each Church accepts full intercommunion with the others and recognizes as valid their ministry and orders.

2. Each Church keeps its specific doctrines.

3. Episcopal succession is extended to all federated Churches. All the Churches of a given territory therefore come under the jurisdiction of one Bishop, who himself may be chosen from a denomination that hitherto excluded episcopacy. All further ordinations will be conferred by those Bishops, but each one is free to understand episcopacy as best he can.

A consequence of this union is that Anglicans of South India practice intercommunion with Churches to which Anglicans of England refuse it. Hence the anomaly that Anglicans are or are not in communion with some Churches, not on account of doctrinal principles, but because of geographic accidents. It is no doubt owing to this strange situation that the Convocations of the Church of England have postponed decision on this point until 1955, when some years of experience may have thrown light on the implications of the South India scheme.

With its subtleties of organization, this method can hardly solve more than superficial difficulties. At its best, it covers up doctrinal divergences with a common experience of brotherly fellowship. At its worst, it dilutes various traditions into a soft-pedaled Christianity.

The idea of joining nonepiscopal Churches under an episcopacy that remains doctrinally ambiguous is, so far, proper to South India, though Ceylon may soon follow suit with a similar, probably improved, plan. Yet a considerable amount of effort on the part of Protestant ecumenists is devoted to the promotion of merger schemes whereby several Churches that are somehow related as to faith and order decide to federate. Between 1938 and 1951, such unions were adopted in Japan, North India, Rhodesia, the Philippines, Germany, and the United States. Closer unions, that abolished a number of Churches in order to form a single one, have been achieved in France, the United States, Switzerland, Holland, Brazil, and Madagascar.[3] It should be noted, however, that the Church of South India stands out as a unique experiment, of interest to missiology no less than to a theology of ecumenism, as it applies to Christian denominations the principle of the identity of opposites as understood in Indian philosophy. Furthermore, the Church of South India cannot be appraised only from the peculiarities of its organization; the implications of its theology must also be considered. For it is giving rise to a relatively new conception of the Church. According to this view the Church should be defined in terms of what it is becoming rather than in terms of what it is. This dynamic approach

[3] Cf. Stephen Neill, *Towards Church Union, 1937-1952.*

may eventually open a way of escape from the difficulties that beset the World Council itself.

This leads to the second kind of attempt at overcoming the doctrinal pluralism of Protestantism. It may be called the way of hope against hope and has been adopted in practice at the great assemblies of the World Council. The message of Amsterdam stated it in clear terms: "We are one in acknowledging Christ as our God and Savior. We are divided from one another not only in matters of faith, order and tradition, but also by pride of nation, class and race. But Christ has made us His own and He is not divided. In seeking Him we find one another." And the following lines may be read in one of the Evanston reports:

We may speak of the oneness of the Church in its earthly pilgrimage as a growth from its unity as given to its unity as fully manifested. In this way we may think of the Church as we are able to think of the individual believer, who may be said at one and the same time to be both a justified man and a sinner (*simul justus et peccator*). . . . So the Church is already one in Christ, by virtue of His identification of Himself with it, and must become one in Christ, so as to manifest its true unity in the mortification of its divisions. Christ of His love and grace has given His Church such gifts as it needs for its growth from unity to unity. . . . The *fact* of our common—though diverse—use of these gifts is a powerful evidence of our unity in Christ and a powerful aid to reminding us that unity lies in His work and not in our own achievements. . . . But the very fact that, in every case, our benefit from these mercies is marred by our separation from each other, compels us now to examine seriously how it is that our disunity as Churches contradicts our oneness in Christ.[4]

These texts imply two points. In the first place the member churches want to unite and remain united; in the second, they are aware of their deep differences. They accordingly consent to disagree on minor points in order to agree on a common faith in Jesus Christ, God and Savior,

---

[4] Report on *Our Oneness in Christ and Our Disunity as Churches.*

and on a mutual respect of differences. Should these divergences not correspond to God's intention, they assume that
God will wipe them out in the future. There is thus a true
structural unity in the ecumenical meetings and a unity in
Christian love. On the level of doctrine, disunity persists
and is provisionally consented to. Each is conscious of remaining faithful to Christ by adhering to a particular tradition in which he sees a witness to a genuine aspect of
Christianity. Each also accepts the fact that other Churches,
through their own denominational loyalty, maintain a
providential constituent of Christianity. How these elements, that are sometimes contradictory, dovetail in the
total Christian synthesis is part of the mystery of God, the
Lord of history, who allowed diverging interpretations to
grow. There is fellowship without perfect unity.

This position is certainly logical; but it is unstable. It is
logical insofar as it takes account of the fact of disunity and
of the peculiar conception of the Church that underlies
Protestant ecumenism. It is nonetheless unstable because it
gives rise to conflicts of loyalty that are not solved by having
recourse to a divine mystery. A comparison of diverging
doctrines is unavoidable and when it is made in earnest it
necessarily leads to an option. Religious experience may no
doubt join what intellectual analysis disjoins. Yet a juxta-
position of diverse doctrines within a common witness
achieves no more than a transitory oneness inside of which
oppositions are not abated. The World Council itself has
indeed attempted to outwit even this ultimate dilemma.
According to the Toronto statement adopted in 1950 by the
Central Committee of the Council, "The World Council
deals in a provisional way with divisions between existing
Churches, which ought not to be, because they contradict
the very nature of the Church. A situation such as this cannot be met in terms of well established precedents. The
main problem is how one can formulate the ecclesiastical
implications of a body in which so many different concep-

tions of the Church are represented, without using the categories or language of one particular conception of the Church." Posited in these terms, the problem can have no solution. The language adopted, for instance, at Evanston tends to show that the World Council is now oriented toward a purely nominal overcoming of doctrinal divergences, by selecting an ambiguous terminology which, as such, is no property of any one doctrinal tradition but may be understood in various senses by all.

This seems to be the present dilemma of Protestant ecumenism.

The Lund meeting, which reached an acute consciousness of the provisional nature of ecumenism, highlighted this dilemma from another angle. Its message urgently insisted that the member churches must not rest satisfied with talk but must express their good will in the domain of hard facts:

We would earnestly request our Churches to consider whether they are doing all they ought to do to manifest the oneness of the people of God. . . . Obedience to God demands also that the Churches seek unity in their mission to the world. . . . The word penitence has been often on our lips here at Lund. Penitence involves willingness to endure judgement—the judgement of the Lord to whom has been given the power to sift mankind and to gather into one the scattered children of God. We await His final triumph at the end of history. But, in God's mercy, tokens of judgement which are also calls to a new and active obedience, come to us in our day also, here and now. Surely we cannot any longer remain blind to the signs of our times and deaf to His Word.

This appeal eloquently points out what knot Protestant ecumenism now has to untie: its doctrinal foundation, without which the World Council could probably not exist any longer, reveals itself inadequate to the requirements of unity such as the New Testament describes it. An English theologian had proposed, though somewhat late, the consideration of another topic, the nontheological factors of disunion. The Lund delegates felt more or less acutely that ecumenism was heading for a dead end. In these circumstances one must regret that they postponed the study of this topic. For it does seem true that the divisions among Christians stem in large part from a real will-to-oppose, which itself originates in sociological and psychological constellations rather than in deeply thought-out doctrinal principles. This holds true even at the crucial points where Protestantism parts from the Catholic Tradition.

Thus to mitigate, inside the Churches, this unconscious though solid adherence to factors of disunion would be for Protestant ecumenism the best way of effectively helping the cause of Christian unity. There is work here for a good many years.

Until this is done, the future development of the ecumenical movement allows of a qualified hope. Yet its very nature as a movement—wherein the relative positions of the member churches evolve with the general development of the whole—makes it particularly sensitive to the numerous influences at large in the Christian world. Its provisional and moving structure opens it to gushes of fresh air that may blow from outside. Among the factors that may wield a healthy influence and contribute to its providential development, Catholicism may become the most vital. This is why the relations between ecumenism and Catholicism call for a detailed study.

Part Two

>>><<<

APPROACHES

Chapter Seven

NEGATIVE ATTITUDES

THERE was a time when anti-Protestant apologetics, in the popularized and falsely scholarly estate to which it is reduced by too many teachers, was an unfortunate mixture of good and not so good. There are still courses that do not venture much further than poking unholy fun at the Protestant Reformation. Such a turn of mind in a would-be professor or writer naturally ought to be alien to any cultured person: it proceeds from a great amount of unintelligence allied to a mountain of ignorance. Reciprocal prejudices have unfortunately been deep enough to give birth to it in some sections of both clergy and laity. This has radically biased the efficiency of Catholicism. For it has given it the appearance of being—contrary to what it really is—another kind of aggressive sectarianism. Luther is then held to be no better than a vulgar lustful monk. Calvin becomes a cruel tyrant. The Anglican Church originates only in Henry VIII's desire to change wives. Every separated Christian body is called a "sect." All religious fervor among non-Catholics looks like fanaticism. Reformed doctrine is reduced to "free interpretation." The history of Protestantism is streamlined into an outline of the "variations of the Protestant Churches" and the persecutions of Catholics. Etc.

This anti-Protestantism is as rabid as it is ignorant. To

the credit of the present century it has been markedly mitigated in the last decades. Yet it is not dead, as witness the
following lines from the preface of a textbook in apologetics
published in 1948:

> At the present moment there is great need for textbooks in
> Christian Apologetics or Evidences. Perhaps there is even greater
> need for texts in Christian Polemics. For it does seem that Catho-
> lics might at last refuse to deal seriously with the insanities charged
> against their religion. It does seem that Catholics might now take
> the active and aggressive stand in the endless argument that goes
> on about their faith; that they might now, after so many, many
> weary refutations of absurdities, require proofs from their op-
> ponents instead of silly charges, and positive doctrine instead of
> the vague sentimentalism and tiresome negations that make up
> the jejune sectarianism of our day. . . . [It would be delightful]
> to charge happily into the part of the "offensive" and turn out a
> textbook that would serve Catholic students by instructing them
> in methods of making the enemies of the true faith consider the
> cheapness and inadequacy of their own resources. . . . The modern
> chapter on the claims of the Catholic Church, as distinct from
> other Christian bodies, may be made much more brief and direct,
> for the simple reason that the "other Christian bodies" have
> largely faded into a vaguely differentiated group with no very
> positive claims of any kind except the general claim to the right
> of taking "centre shots at Rome." . . .[1]

Such an attitude is too overwhelmingly simplified for us
to waste time trying to correct it. It throws contempt on its
author rather than on what it slings mud at. And yet—
which is no less than a catastrophe—it goes on spreading
among Catholics and others a thousand mistaken ideas,
wrong judgments, and prejudices that are beyond uproot-
ing. There is no cause for surprise, then, that peace among
Christians does not yet belong to our era.

The negative attitudes occasionally adopted toward Protestants are far from being all reduced to a nauseating igno-

[1] Paul Glenn, *Apologetics,* pp. v-vii.

rance. We have also to take account of some infinitely nobler positions, that call for respect even where one should disagree with them. These have at times been upheld by some of the greatest names in modern Catholicism.

Let us mention first of all what may be termed a romantic apologetics. What it tends to call Protestantism is not Protestantism itself as a historical religious fact. It is rather an abstract interpretation of that fact. No idyllic picture of the Reformation is drawn: on the contrary, its defects are overstressed. A romantic view of Catholicism itself, however, brings in a slanted interpretation of Protestantism.

The Reformation is not judged on the historical background of the sixteenth century, as an event which was first of all conditioned by the decay of Christendom at the time. From the vantage point of the eternal Church, of the continuing mission of the mystical Body on this earth, of the splendor of the theoretical and practical role played by the Papacy in the formation of Western culture, the Reformation is seen, through a sort of metaphysical vision which dominates history, as the most successful work of Satan. No doubt, one remembers that the fifteenth- and sixteenth-century Church needed reform "in the head and the limbs," that its current theology was no longer that of the great doctors and Fathers, that deep corruption went often side by side with high holiness. These facts, however, are pushed into the background or even brushed aside as accidental occasions that cannot account for what goes on in the underworld, where heresies and revolts are planned out in the evil mind of the demons. At most they can explain, in this view, why the Reformation was so successful with princes and people and how the Protestant upheaval differed in degree and nature from hundreds of minor or major heresies that had cropped up before. In this supposed titanic struggle between light and darkness, Catholicism itself does not figure as the Church in her God-given mission, as the mystical Body of Christ unfolding itself in the course of time, but rather as the accidental influence of the Church over the development of culture and civilization. Besides an injustice toward the Reformation and a mistreatment of facts, this necessarily implies a real devaluation of Catholicism, which loses its transcendence when its influence on the formation of cultures and societies is overemphasized. Its universality is also strait-jacketed by undertones that tend so to associate "Europe and the faith" (this is the title of a book by Hilaire Belloc) that Catholicism becomes exclusively European and, at a still more devalued stage, merely Western and "Latin."

One of the most striking examples of this tendency is no other than the famous book of the great Jaime Balmes, *El Protestantismo comparado con el Catolicismo* (1842-1844). This remarkable work has valuable insights into some secondary aspects of Protestantism and provides magnificent vistas on Catholicism as a factor of true progress and real culture. Yet it utterly misunderstands the tragic nature of the Reformation. From the standpoint he had adopted, Balmes simply could not see into the Protestant mind. The religious profundity of Luther and his followers is bound to be overlooked when one chooses to view Protestantism as only an unwontedly acute crisis in a permanent revolt against God's authority. Balmes thought that a history of human pride could be traced alongside the development of the Church. But this is not at all the Protestant dilemma. The drama of the sixteenth century lies precisely in the co-existence of a seldom equaled religious depth and of a conviction of being driven to leave the Church in order to remain faithful to conscience and to one's apprehension of the greatness and transcendence of God. When the core of Protestantism, which is so rich and varied for those who are acquainted with it, is reduced to a "dissolving principle" which annihilates all positive beliefs, the true meaning of the Protestant protest is missed. One becomes unable to perceive the basic fidelity harbored in the Protestant soul.

Starting from such a misreading of the basic pattern of Protestantism, Balmes can easily "demonstrate" that Protestantism undermines the very foundations of European civilization, that the Catholic Church alone has contributed to its
vitality, and that non-Catholic influence has been systematically negative. Such a demonstration is sheer wishful thinking. And the great mind that Balmes undoubtedly was would
have been the first to notice it had he only studied Protestantism with a serious historical method rather than by
throwing on it the sidelights of a romantic vision of Europe
and perhaps even of the Church.

This sort of apologetics flourished in the last century,
though—as we shall see—it never was universal. Clear
traces of it are to be found, not only in the works of Balmes,
but in those of some of the greatest names in French Catholicism, like the de Maistre brothers, Emmanuel d'Alzon, or
Louis Veuillot. It is far from dead at the present time. One
has only to go through the writings of Hilaire Belloc to be
struck by that identification of Europe with the faith. Name-
calling transforms the Reformation into one phase of mankind's perennial revolt against authority. Protestantism in
general is denounced as the enemy of culture and modern
Protestantism in particular as a lifeless body that would
have nothing to bring to civilization.

This shortsighted apologetical method is not special to
Catholics. Protestantism also has known that kind of apol-
ogists. Which goes to show that whatever side it sponsors,
its arguments leave plenty of probability to the opposite
side.

We now come to a much more theological approach,
which is more objective in its knowledge of facts, less one-
sided in its judgments of value, yet radically biased in its
methods, sometimes uncharitable in its choice of adjectives,
and all the more dangerous as it advertises itself more
openly as the self-styled champion of doctrinal orthodoxy.

This should not be misunderstood. We are now dealing with men who wish to be true theologians and apostles of Christian unity, who have perceived the existence of Protestantism as a call or a vocation to help span the chasm over which the Protestant mind has to travel before reaching again the one Church of Christ. Yet they start on this work with a number of assumptions that lead them to harm rather than to help their cause. This they do with the best intentions in the world and without being aware of it. This peculiar mentality may be compared with what is called in some countries "integralism." Integralism in this sense is a view of the truth which leads to defend the contents of the Catholic faith in a sort of desperate fashion, as when soldiers have been pushed back to their last ditch and have to fight or die: then delay becomes treason and soft-handed tactics are highly imprudent. It is a question of nervousness and unsettled temper perhaps as much as of bad theology.[2]

When it deals with problems of Christian unity, this attitude is a most strange phenomenon, since, unselfishly and unwittingly, it becomes unfit to fulfill the generous task it has assigned to itself. Elements of that approach may be easily described.

A theological method of thinking proceeds, as St. Thomas says, *ex auctoritate*.[3] Another ecclesiastical discipline, Canon Law, also argues *ex auctoritate*. But instead of being concerned with doctrine, it studies, compares, and explains the decisions of a mainly disciplinary character taken by the constituted authority in the Church. The confusion between Canon Law and theology often entails a misunderstanding of the aims and methods of Catholic ecumenism. Thus, wishing to study "the reunion of Christendom," according to the documents of the Holy See, a recent author

[2] On the evils attached to integralism, cf. *The Church Today. Collected writings of Emmanuel Cardinal Suhard*, pp. 131-137.
[3] *S. T.*, I, p. 1, a. 8, ad. 2.

takes as his starting point a distinction between what he terms divine Revelation (that is, Scripture and Tradition) and divine authority, identified with the "approval of the Holy See."[4] His argumentation then leaves aside Scripture and Tradition and attaches itself to discovering what method of reunion has met with the approval of the Holy See. After citing a number of texts, the meaning of which is not even analyzed, the author imagines he is in a position to provide a fair account of Catholic ecumenism. Yet his reader is enlightened neither on the thought of the Popes nor on the theological implications of the problem under survey, simply because a method that argues merely from disciplinary documents is not a theological method.

This basic misconception all but necessarily entails overstatements as regards the meaning of the texts adduced. Quoted without any reference to their historical or textual setting, excerpts from pontifical documents are unduly transformed into pieces of machinery seemingly extracted from a vast polemical contrivance. Thus, having read in the encyclical *Humani Generis* that one must avoid a dangerous irenicism, another writer boldly concludes: "This Apostolic letter puts forth in no uncertain terms the attitude that is to be taken by the Catholic Bishops of the Universal Church as well as Catholic theologians and philosophers in regard to ecumenical movements such as the *Universal Week of Prayer for Christian Unity*."[5] Thus misrepresented, the encyclical is made to appear as condemning a practice which is in reality sponsored by a multitude of Bishops. A small amount of well-balanced moderation would have shown that the irenicism listed in the encyclical has nothing to do with a pious practice like the Week of Prayer for Christian Unity. Underlying such a misuse of pontifical texts one may sometimes discern a fundamental error on the function of the Papacy in the Church. Thus Father Hanahoe elimi-

---

[4] E. F. Hanahoe, *Catholic Ecumenism*, p. 44.
[5] David Gannon, *Father Paul of Graymoor*, p. 277. (Italics original.)

nates from theology the notion of *vestigia ecclesiae,* for the alleged reason that "there is no justification to be found in Papal documents" for such a doctrine.[6] In sober fact, the work of theologians is one thing, and the task of the Supreme Pontiff another. The latter has the clear duty to warn the former against occasional imprudences or even slanted positions. He is bound now and again to put an end to theological debates or even philosophical discussions that touch on matters of faith. Yet it is not in his function as Pontiff to proceed himself to the pioneer work of research, reflection, patient deciphering of documents, and system-building, which is the work of theologians. When some theologians are led to remark that the full Catholic Tradition implies, for instance, a doctrine on the "remains of the Church" that are still alive in schismatic or heretic bodies, the silence of modern pontifical statements simply shows that the Roman Pontiff has enough to do with his governing and guiding function. Any other conclusion would derive from a loaded argument. Yet it is proper to the turn of mind in question that it is never satisfied with something that has not yet been included in an encyclical. Now, except in notable instances, the theology of the encyclicals, of its very nature, is no more than the doctrine which is commonly agreed upon in the various Catholic schools, accompanied with the wise caution that goes with the universal teaching responsibility in the Church. To limit theological research to culling pontifical texts would amount to putting a premature end to the search after the intellection of faith which presided over the great theological eras of the Patristic times and the Middle Ages. As for those who do not rest content with quotations, but replace them with what they wrongly imagine is their sense, they simply stand outside intellectual honesty.

This approach to ecumenical problems is often developed side by side with a certain highhandedness toward those

6 *Op. cit.,* p. 101.

who do not stand on exactly the same ground. A few lines then suffice to wipe away the patient, faithful, and serene work of theologians of note. Fathers Victor White and Yves Congar are thus annihilated.[7] The generous and tragic vision of Abbé Portal is misjudged as a "virtual denial of the ecumenical mission of the Church of Christ."[8] The Malines conversations are pronounced a failure, owing to the fact that "continental Catholics were especially unsuited to the handling of the Anglican question,"[9] as though historical and doctrinal competence were a matter of geography. This intellectual pettiness naturally does not stop short when it has misjudged opinions and men. It furthermore (and one cannot see how things could turn out differently) slants our own outlook, so that the facts that will provide us with points of departure or support are not the facts themselves as they took place: they are rather what our confused mind has reduced them to.

This defect is obvious in a number of ready-made assertions concerning separated Christians. If one quality may be required of Catholic ecumenists, it is, at least, fact-finding objectivity. This needs infinite patience, the power to reserve judgment, steadiness in examining all the circumstances of a case, mastery over one's pet ideas and wishes. Never to fall short of, or reach beyond, what documents allow; never unduly to squeeze the meaning of things and words; not to take right away the terms used by separated Christians at what is their face value for a Catholic; to force oneself to be at home in a spiritual and intellectual world where one does not belong; to follow its hurdle-jumping and its slow sidetracking of problems—all this is difficult to achieve. Moreover, theologians cannot be improvised at random; and who would venture unprepared in the field of ecumenical theology would risk falling into rash judg-

[7] *Ibid.*, pp. 100-101.
[8] *Ibid.*, p. 146.
[9] *Ibid.*, p. 136.

ments all day long. Yet much writing on Protestantism is at the exact opposite of those needed qualities and piles up misinformation as to facts and mistreatment as to opinions.

This tendency to disregard theological equity when one deals with Protestants sometimes reaches elephantine dimensions. It even entails an active hostility to the Christian elements of Protestantism. It seems—this is a matter of history—that Cardinal Wiseman somehow persuaded himself that Newman's conversion had been due, among other factors, to his own unbendingness toward the Tractarians. He in fact put down a principle that could serve as the motto of integralism in ecumenical questions: "To have allowed it [the Anglican Establishment] to possess a single mark or element of catholicity . . . would have been both false in theology and pernicious in practise. It would have encouraged a fatal delusion, which, undisturbed, might have laid many asleep in a fatal contentment, who now repose in peaceful security in the bosom of their Mother, the Church. No real love for those involved in this state could be shown, except by energetic endeavors to snatch them from it. Whoever therefore wished to be truly their best friend had to make up his mind to appear their most unrelenting opponent."[10] In other words, the best means to bring all Anglicans back to Holy Church would consist in driving the Anglican Establishment as far away from Catholicism as possible. As for the properly Protestant denominations, it would be best to make them as "liberal" as they could possibly become. Through strangely twisted thinking, the conclusion is thus reached that the more indifference or downright paganism harbored in Protestantism, the better the opportunity to unite Christendom. It is a weird method—yet an easy escape from responsibilities—which solves a problem by spiriting away the data! Clearly enough, once all non-Catholic Christians have turned into, say, Buddhists, the ecumenical question is no longer posited.

[10] *Essays on Various Subjects,* 1853, Vol. II, pp. vii-viii.

With this assumption more or less consciously admitted, too many work in fact against the positive Christian values that the Reformation has preserved to this day. The tragedy is that they do it with concern for Christian unity and in the name of charity! Every Catholic will promptly acquiesce in the statement that "no better service to these dissidents could be given than to offer them a clear and unequivocal declaration of our position."[11] Yet this has to be done without misrepresenting facts and doctrines. To give an example, it is untrue to facts to write: "Basically and essentially they [the 'Anglo-Catholics'] are Protestants, who, through private judgement, have arrived at some approximation of Catholic doctrine, and, through liberal borrowings, have assumed a certain external resemblance to Catholic ritual. Needless to say, these act on their own judgement in opposition to their own religious ordinances and the will of their officials."[12] To underestimate non-Catholic Christians in an attempt to make our task easier is a kind of apologetical duplicity that runs foul of the truth. It is not compatible with a Catholic ecumenism or, simply, with mere honesty.

Opposite to this sort of inverted ecumenism, we have now to mention the irenicism which the encyclical *Humani Generis* pointed out to theologians as unsafe. We can be short here, since the next chapter will survey Roman documents. The encyclical is devoted to listing the dangers that are run when one tries strenuously to adapt the Church to the modern world through some sort of leveling down that would erase partitions and achieve the union of all in a common good will. No irenic approach to problems of a divided Christendom may be attempted if it also damages the unchanging structure of the Church or the fullness of Revelation.

[11] Hanahoe, op. cit., p. 13.
[12] *Ibid.*, p. 138.

It is of course not excluded that such a kind of exaggeration can at times arise among Catholic ecumenists who are more well meaning than farsighted. Yet the encyclical does not refer to them in particular. It rather implicitly aims at them in warning against a more general peril. Catholic thinkers cannot close their ears to the modern call to economic, political, and cultural unity. In their well-intended desire to understand the modern world, to place the Church among the pioneers of a new type of civilization, to turn Catholicism into the driving force of humanity as it was that of Europe in the past, they may be attracted by a generous conception of religious unity and may dream of sloughing off antiquated forms of thought or outmoded methods of apostolate. So far so good. Thence to label "relative" the structure and doctrine of the Church, there is a sizable distance, which excessive or badly enlightened minds may, however, too quickly cover. Among the apostles of the twentieth century thus advised to stave off a powerful and wily temptation there may be laborers in the field of Catholic ecumenism: this is to be expected and feared.

Humani Generis thus pointed to a barrier not to be trespassed over. For those who were well versed in theology and well read in history, however, the barrier was already erected. As is his function, the Holy Father brought it into better light: the theologian and apostle of ecumenism simply must, like every other theologian and apostle, remain faithful to Catholic truth and walk along the safe path of intellectual and practical prudence.

Chapter Eight

OFFICIAL PRONOUNCEMENTS

THE ATTITUDE adopted by the Holy See as regards separated Churches has been described and justified in a long series of documents published since the time of the Reformation when occasion called for it. Protestantism, Anglicanism, and the movements that branched off from them constitute what Canon Law must call heresies and schisms. The Supreme Pontiffs can hardly do more than express regret for their past separation and encourage them to take steps that will eventually make their return possible. The words "heresy" and "schism" may be understood in a material and a formal sense. The latter sense is verified when a material error concerning the object of faith or a breach of Christian fellowship is accompanied by a subjectively grave sin. Yet since no single man is able to pass judgment on his neighbor and since, according to moralists and canonists, the Church herself does not judge what is purely interior to a conscience, the formal meaning of these terms is usually excluded from pontifical documents. Considered as abstract entities, the separated Churches are condemned; but the conscience of their members is respected. One ought therefore to be very careful when trying to interpret the canonical meaning of the expressions used in official documents of the Church and avoid hurting with, or being hurt by, them, as though they were ever meant as insults. An overstressing of the canonical vocabulary in a sense which is far from canonical remains to this day a too frequent abuse. It results in an exchange of injustice on one side and resentment on the other.

One should not imagine, either, that pontifical texts and the documents coming from the various offices of the Holy See hide, under the cloak of apparently harmless sentences, a sort of secret meaning wherein those who are privy to it may discern mysterious and usually evil intentions. As though the Church were no other than a political tool in the hands of a gang called—in certain quarters—the "Vatican State"! This misconstruction of texts, which is common in some secular or even Protestant circles, is simply a historical nonsense. Thus the condemnation of Anglican orders (pronounced by Leo XIII in his Apostolic Letter *Apostolicae Curae* in 1896) is still sometimes resented as though it had been an arbitrary measure adopted with the sole aim of knocking down the Anglican communion. As a matter of fact, this condemnation—which was a disciplinary decision taken after a responsible historical study of the question—must be understood against the background of the encyclical *Satis Cognitum,* published some months before by the same Pontiff. This is an altogether remarkable document, which expounds the traditional doctrine on the unity of the Holy Catholic and Apostolic Church and puts down, among other remarks, a prudential principle that will justify the condemnation of Anglican orders: "Such is the nature of faith that nothing can be more absurd than to accept some things and reject others." Since the Holy Father cannot view the Anglican Church or the other separated bodies otherwise than as abstract entities, he does not stop to consider—as he would have to do if he were speaking of individual human beings—that the strangely twisted psychology of man is quite able to erect an "absurdity" inside faith itself. And he is naturally led to conclude that the rejection of a part of Tradition vitiated all the litur-

gical works of the English Reformers and implied a re-
nunciation of the Catholic intention of "doing what the
Church does" in ordinations and consecrations. To the
mind of Leo XIII himself, the ensuing condemnation was
intended to clarify pending questions and get rid of false
or unessential problems. As it is, the two encyclicals *Satis
Cognitum* and *Apostolicae Curae* were published between
two Apostolic Letters—May 5, 1895, and May 9, 1897—in
which Leo XIII inaugurated and recommended the practice, all but forgotten these days, of devoting the novena
before Pentecost to prayer for Christian unity. The Pope's
mind was thus formulated in the second letter: "We have
desired that all the works undertaken and pursued in the
course of an already long pontificate aim at two main ends:
first, at a restoration of Christian life in society and family,
among princes as well as among the people, for all true
life derives from Christ; afterwards, at a reconciliation of
all who are separated from the Church on questions of faith
or jurisdiction, for it most certainly is Christ's intention to
unite them in one fold under one shepherd."

Who truly wants to understand the policy of the Holy
See regarding, for instance, the modern ecumenical movement should accordingly keep two points in mind. In the
first place, he ought to take account of the simplicity and
straightforwardness of the canonical language and give up
interpretations that do not fit with the concrete doctrinal
and historical context of that language. In the second place,
he has to attune himself to a vision of the separated
Churches. Because keeping the principles of the faith is its
special duty, the Apostolic See does not leave the realm of
principles. It therefore views non-Catholic communions as
abstract entities rather than as believing communities where
millions of men undergo a profound, if incomplete or
slanted, experience of Christianity.

The papal documents on Christian unity that have been
published since the beginning of the great ecumenical con-

ferences of the present century may be divided into three kinds, which correspond to three successive moments in the cautious and sound, if slow, formation of an official Catholic attitude toward Protestant ecumenism. The first attempts by the organizers of *Faith and Order* and *Life and Work* to enlist the participation of the Catholic Church met with a courteous, but unequivocal, refusal. There should be no cause for surprise in this. For the Holy See cannot afford to become reckless. The greatness of the doctrinal Tradition it carries along forces it to be cautious in the domain of what may be called ecclesiastical policy. Now, in the twenties nobody knew what would come out of the efforts of the pioneers of ecumenism in the Protestant world. These pioneers themselves were aware of groping in the dark. They felt somehow urged to go on, but they could not be sure where their initiative would lead or even that it would lead anywhere at all. Besides unavoidably obscure points in their projects there was an undeniable theological confusion as to the doctrinal principles involved. Things could hardly have happened otherwise in those truly heroic years. Yet in these conditions the idea that the Holy See could share in those tentative efforts proceeded from a certain misconception of the situation of the Papacy in the modern world. The structure of present-day society, with its social and cultural pluralism, its separation of the secular and the religious, presents a definite obstacle to the Papacy's participation in movements whose ambiguous constituents place them under the sway of the sociological laws that form and shuffle public opinion. Like every other institution, the Papacy must remain faithful to its structure and history. The sacral Christendom of the Middle Ages did not present the same kind of obstacle, precisely because the framework of its society followed other laws. When the heyday of the Middle Ages was over, the Papacy kept its old practice of directly stepping down into the arena of secular politics. But the changing world was no longer ready for that; and the Papacy went through its greatest crisis in history and learned an unforgotten lesson. The too optimistic flavor of *Life and Work* looked too much like the corresponding atmosphere of the League of Nations. The implications of *Faith and Order* mixed too many concerns for expediency with doctrinal principles. This naturally awakened a distrust that had been born of experience and that the relatively recent episode of "modernism" had rendered more sensitive than ever.

The Holy See not only stayed aside. It also forbade Catholics to join the movement on their own responsibility. A few weeks before the Lausanne Conference a decree from the Holy Office—July 8, 1927—gave a negative answer to the following question: "Are Catholics allowed to attend conferences, meetings, assemblies or associations of non-Catholics that have as their aim that all who claim the name of Christian be united together with one religious link, or to sponsor such organizations?" Some months later—January 2, 1928—the encyclical *Mortalium Animos* was devoted to the movement for Christian reunion. When we read this encyclical today, we are struck by the fact that it can hardly square with what we now know as the ecumenical movement. It does not aim at what the movement has turned into. It rather draws attention to what one could fear, in the circumstances of 1927-1928, that it would become. What His Holiness Pius XI discerned in the undertones and assumptions of the movement, as they could be perceived in the exchanges of views of Stockholm and Lausanne, was no other than a new form of the so-called "modernism" which had caused trouble at the turn of the twentieth century.

Passages like the following take their full value in this perspective: "Assured that there exist few men who are entirely devoid of the religious sense, they seem to ground on this belief a hope that all nations, while differing indeed in religious matters, may yet without great difficulty be brought to fraternal agreement on certain points of doctrine

which will form a common basis of the spiritual life . . . .
[Such efforts] presuppose the erroneous view that all religions are more or less good and praiseworthy, inasmuch as
all give expression, under various forms, to that innate sense
which leads men to God and to the obedient acknowledge-
ment of His rule. Those who hold such a view are not only
in error; they distort the true idea of religion, and thus reject it, falling gradually into naturalism and atheism. To
favor this opinion therefore, and to encourage such under-
takings is tantamount to abandoning the religion revealed by
God." Looked at carefully, the key words of this text have an
unmistakable "modernist" flavor: "common basis of the
spiritual life," "all religions more or less good and praiseworthy," "innate sense which leads men to God," "abandoning the religion revealed by God."

Having in mind this possible threat of a new "modernism," the Pope then speaks explicitly of the movement
for Christian unity: "These and similar arguments, with
amplifications, are constantly on the lips of the 'pan-Christians' who, so far from being isolated individuals, have
formed an entire class and grouped themselves into societies
of extensive membership, usually under the direction of
non-Catholics, who also disagree in matters of faith . . . .
In reality however, these fair and alluring words cloak a
most grave error, subversive of the foundations of the Catholic faith." Further on Pius XI warns against "schemes for
the promiscuous union into one body of all who call themselves Christians." As the Pope sees it, the idea of those
"pan-Christians" is that "from the residue of doctrines a
common form of faith [must be] drawn up and proposed
for belief, in the profession of which all may not only know
but also feel themselves to be brethren. . . ." The Pope
adds: "We do know that from such a state of affairs it is but
an easy step to the neglect of religion or 'indifferentism,'
and to the error of the modernists, who hold that dogmatic
truth is not absolute but relative, that is, that it changes

according to the varying necessities of time and place and
the varying tendencies of the mind; that it is not contained
in an immutable tradition, but can be altered to suit the
needs of human life."

If indeed Protestant ecumenism was that (and who in
1928 could be certain it was not?) the conclusion was in-
escapable: "This being so, it is clear that the Apostolic See
can by no means take part in these assemblies, nor is it in
any way lawful for Catholics to give to such enterprises their
encouragement and support. If they did so, they would be
giving countenance to a false Christianity quite alien to the
one church of Christ."

Many Protestants who were deeply Christian and unaffected by "modernism"—"modernism" had been, in its
acute form, a Catholic rather than a Protestant phenomenon
—were hurt by the encyclical *Mortalium Animos*. We can
still find the attitude of the Holy See summed up with the
truncated quotation: the ecumenical movement is "subversive of the foundations of the Catholic faith." In reality
the encyclical has an utterly different meaning when this
expression is read in its true context: what is "subversive of
the foundations of the Catholic faith" is by no means the
ecumenical movement as it now exists but the modernist
tendency which the Holy See, rightly or wrongly, perceived
in some aspects of it, and which is now, to a large extent,
subdued. The doctrinal value of *Mortalium Animos* remains
unimpaired to this day, since it does no more than re-express
the perennial assertions of the Catholic Tradition transmitted and developed through the ages. Yet insofar as it
tries to identify "pan-Christianity" with the ecumenical
movement its interest is now mainly historical. A new situation calls for a reappraisal: ecumenism now cannot be
equated with the "pan-Christianity" rightly condemned by
Pius XI. It is not grounded in the idea of dogmatic relativity,
but in an affirmation of the mystery of the Church whose
function is to witness to Christ in spite of divergences

between denominations that are maintained in conscience at the very moment when they are regretted. Each one trusts that his basic conceptions are right; but all bow to the transcendence of the Church. All hope that a day will come when the mystery of the Church will absorb divergences, through the gratuitous workings of God.

In these conditions, and since new questions were thus posited to the Catholic conscience, the Holy See has been brought to adopt a new attitude.

The war years 1939-1945 were for the World Council of Churches a period of silent reflection and waiting. The same years saw the Holy Father come out again and again in favor of a coöperation between all the men who are united in faith in God and, still more forcefully, all who share faith in Christ. Whereas the World Council, that was still in its formative period, was more often than not reduced to working underground, the ecumenical concerns of the Supreme Pontiff were seen more and more in the open. Besides knowing himself to be the leader of the Church as a visible institution, Pius XII renewed the great tradition, according to which the Church has to assume in herself all mankind and her visible head to guide all men to salvation. In the words of the Christmas message of the Pope for 1940, "The Church. . . , the common Mother of all men, perceives and understands better than anybody the aspiration that spontaneously arises from the tormented soul of mankind." On this general theme, it was natural that Pius XII should seek to reach separated Christians.

The very day following his election, the Pope declared, "Our thought also goes to all who are outside the fold of the Catholic Church. We trust that they also will gladly know that in this solemn moment we beseech the all-bounteous and almighty God to grant them His divine assistance . . . . We truly entertain the firm hope that you, our sons, and you, our brothers, will not bring to nought our most burning wish to ensure peace."[1] He also wrote a few months later: "We do not wish to omit a mention of the echo of warm gratitude that has been awakened in our hearts by the congratulations of those who, although they do not belong to the visible body of the Catholic Church, did not forget, in the nobility and sincerity of their feelings, all that unites them to us both in love for the Person of Christ and in faith in God. May the expression of our gratefulness go to them all! We entrust them, each and all, to the protection and leadership of the Lord, and we give them the solemn guarantee that only one thought prevails in our mind: carefully to imitate the Good Shepherd to lead all men to true happiness, so that they may have life and have it abundantly."[2]

The numerous messages of the Supreme Pontiff during World War II outlined a program for a peace achieved in justice. This program significantly envisioned the common good of nations independently of their religious orientations, on the basis of the natural law and the law of nations. In order to reach such an aim, the Pope called on "all who are united to us through the bonds of faith" (Christmas, 1939), "all who, without belonging to the visible body of the Catholic Church, are near to us through faith in God and Jesus Christ, and are in agreement with us as to the organization and the aims of peace" (Christmas, 1941).

Taking account of the cultural and religious pluralism of modern society, Pius XII drew the following conclusion: "The more and more frequent contacts and the disparate mixture of various religious confessions within one people have brought civil law courts to adopt the principle of tolerance and freedom of conscience. In this fact, furthermore, there is a political, civil and social tolerance concerning the faithful of other religions which is also for Catholics, in those circumstances, a moral duty."[3] More

---

[1] *Dum Gravissimum,* March 3, 1939.
[2] *Summi Pontificatus,* October 20, 1939.
[3] Address to the members of the Roman Rota, October 6, 1946.

recently the Holy Father added: "The obligation of re-
pressing errors of ethics and religion cannot be an ultimate
norm of behavior. It must be subordinate to higher and
more general norms which in some circumstances permit,
and sometimes even show as being more perfect, the tolerance of error in view of a higher good."[4] The peaceful
coexistence of religious confessions in a society organized
on the principle of the common good of public order and
social justice is founded on the primary unity of men in
the creative act of God and the redemptive actions of Jesus
Christ: "The only firm basis for the harmony of this world
is this essential union which already binds all men together
by the fact that their God and Creator is their sole common Father in heaven, He who gave His only Son for the
redemption of all, from first to last. The mission of the
Church is to hasten in the day when this truth will be
universally acknowledged. All our life and each of our
days are thoroughly devoted to attaining to this end."[5]

The great task of world unity cannot bring the Supreme
Pontiff to overlook the unique role of the Catholic Church.
Hence the Pope's appeal to separated Christians to join
the one fold again. One of the aims assigned to the Holy
Year 1950 was precisely that "those who do not yet know
Catholic truth . . . be illuminated by supernatural light";[6]
and the Bull *Munificentissimus Deus* of November 1, 1950,
listing the motives that made advisable a definition of the
Assumption, asserted: "There is good ground to hope . . .
that all who make their boast of the name of Christ will
long more fervently to be united with the Mystical Body.
. . ." Since, contrary to the Pope's expectations, the definition was rather unwelcome in non-Catholic circles, his
Christmas message for 1950 voiced a new call to Christian
brotherhood: "On this occasion we deliberately omit to

[4] Address to the Union of Italian Catholic lawyers, December 6, 1953.
[5] Address to some American Senators, October 27, 1949.
[6] *Jubilaeum Maximum*, May 26, 1949.

mention some disagreements which recently arose between Catholics and the members of other religious societies and which have, in part and very inopportunely, penetrated the field of political discussions. We wish to hope that outside of those polemics that are irksome no less than harmful, there will be found in all non-Catholic circles men and women of good will who, rightly concerned with the dangers that now threaten the sacred legacy of the Christian faith, will foster in their hearts other thoughts than thoughts of disunion and discord among brothers."

The pontifical line of thought clearly takes account of both the fact of Christian disunity as regards the development of doctrine and the other fact of the basic union of Christians in faith and charity. It accordingly insists that one should maintain and reinforce what unites rather than what keeps asunder. For even when men are separated from the "visible body of the Church," their essential oneness in the order of creation is enhanced and strengthened by Christian unity in faith and charity. It serves also as a pointer on the road leading to perfect unity in the "visible body of the Church." Thus Pius XII invoked the Blessed Virgin Mary more recently: "May the same Blessed Virgin Mary look down on all those who are proud to call themselves Christian, and who, being united at least by the bond of charity, humbly raise to her their eyes, their minds and their prayers, imploring that light which illumines the mind with heavenly rays, and begging for that unity by which at last there may be one fold and one shepherd."[7]

A fair assessment of the attitude of the Papacy in respect to the ecumenical movement cannot overlook—yet the contrary seems to be the rule in ecumenical literature—this significant development of the concerns of the Supreme Pontiff. The cause of Christian unity as bringing to perfection the unity of the world provides one of the basic intentions that inspire the actions of Pius XII. Even when

[7] *Fulgens Corona,* September 8, 1953.

they consider themselves in duty bound to disagree with some of those stands, Protestants and especially the leaders of the World Council cannot in all fairness ignore this aspect of the modern Papacy. Granted that the methods and, to a certain extent, the principles differ, they themselves wish to make the ecumenical movement into an efficient factor of Christian peace among men and nations. On diverse roads the visible head of the Catholic Church and the leaders of the main separated Churches have thus reached one and the same conclusion, namely, that for the present day Christian unity has a rarely equaled urgency and that accordingly, alongside the obstacles that cannot yet be superseded, one ought to bolster up existing factors of unity.

The problem therefore consists in finding in what measure Catholics and Protestants can work together to that common end. What attitude has the Holy See adopted toward the contemporary ecumenical movement?

On July 12, 1939, the Apostolic Delegate in Great Britain wrote to the Anglican Archbishop of York, in the name of the Cardinal Secretary of State: "There is no obstacle in the way of consultation with the Bishops and the Apostolic Delegate. Likewise there is nothing in the way of exchange of confidential information with Catholic theologians, who will, naturally, make reply in their own name."[8] The attempts made by the organizers of the Amsterdam Assembly to insure the presence of Catholic theologians who would speak on their own responsibility rather than in any official capacity ran foul of the decrees of the Holy Office of June, 1948. The nature of the assembly, however, and the seemingly great number of Catholics who wished to attend did not exactly cover what was understood by "an exchange of confidential information." The slowdown movement then maneuvered by the Holy See corresponded

[8] G. K. Bell, *Documents on Christian Unity,* 3rd series, no. 220.

therefore to a situation that called for particular caution.[9]

On September 20, 1949, another document was issued, which well reflects the outstanding features of ecumenism as it now is and takes full account of the precisions to be added to the cautious view of the situation that had prevailed with Pius XI in 1928.

While maintaining the principle that the Church does not participate in "ecumenical conventions and other assemblies" and pointing out the possible danger of doctrinal indifference which is latent in all religious organizations where various beliefs meet on an equal footing, the Holy Office speaks of the intrinsic value of the ecumenical movement: "In several parts of the world, either on account of world events and a change in interior dispositions, or mainly because of the common prayer of the faithful, the desire has become daily more acute in the hearts of many men separated from the Catholic Church, under the inspiration of the grace of the Holy Spirit, that all who believe in Christ Our Lord should return to unity. This is for the children of the true Church a source of holy joy in the Lord and an invitation to help those who sincerely search for the truth by beseeching God through fervent prayers to grant them the necessary light and strength." The Catholic hierarchy has a duty toward this movement: "Since this reunion comes first of all within the function and duty of the Church, the Bishops, 'that the Holy Ghost has established to govern the Church of God,' must look after it with special care. Not only must they diligently and efficiently watch over all that movement, they must furthermore promote and direct it with prudence, first to help those who seek after the truth, and also to warn off

[9] One may also find in H. S. Leiper, *Relations Between the Ecumenical Movement and the Vatican in the Twentieth Century*, pp. 11-27, interesting details on the strange activity of Mr. Myron Taylor, personal representative of President Truman to the Vatican, during the months that preceded the Amsterdam Assembly.

from the faithful dangers that easily result from the activity of the movement."

The Holy See envisions no adherence to the World Council of Churches, but rather an influence of the Catholic hierarchy on the general orientation of the movement. This influence should follow from the attention and care brought to it by the Bishops and the way they try to promote and direct it.

In practice the Holy Office would advocate colloquies between Catholic and non-Catholic theologians, the local Bishop being active in them through being kept informed of all that concerns the movement in his diocese and through his efforts to have Catholic doctrine explained without watering down, as against the indifferentism that Pius XI feared. Practical rules on the organization of such meetings are not relevant to our purpose here. Yet we may stress the insistence of the Holy See on this aspect of the episcopal function: "In order that this splendid task of the reunion of all Christians in the one true faith and the one true Church may day by day become more and more a select part of the universal care of souls and that all the Catholic lay people may ask more fervently from God this return to unity, it will certainly be useful to acquaint the faithful in a suitable manner, for instance through pastoral letters, with these problems and efforts, the rulings of the Church in these matters and the reasons that inspire them."

When the encyclical *Humani Generis* was published in August, 1950, some unadvised readers thought they could identify the "irenicism" it warned against, with every approach to the ecumenical movement. As we have seen, this interpretation can be called fanciful. The irenicism involved certainly covers the possible indifferentism which could creep into a theology of ecumenism; yet the encyclical by no means withdraws from the positions adopted by the Holy Office in its 1949 Instruction. As a point of fact, when the *Faith and Order* commission met at Lund in 1952, four Catholic observers nominated by the Vicar Apostolic in Sweden attended the conference as "accredited visitors." The Lutheran Archbishop of Upsala, Yngve Brilioth, welcomed them with these words:

That the Church of Rome has not found it possible to take active part in any of the gatherings which we have been used to call ecumenical in spite of the absence of so large a part of the Christian world, is a tragic fact which we have had to accept. That for the first time Roman Catholic observers have been appointed, by due authority, is an important sign that the great Church of Rome is not indifferent to what is being done in order to further a better understanding between Christians of different traditions, and that an amity of souls can exist in spite of ecclesiastical barriers that appear insurmountable. I have great pleasure in welcoming the observers who have been appointed by the Vicar Apostolic of Stockholm.

The impression of Yngve Brilioth is right. It clearly follows from our survey of official documents of the Holy See in the last decades that "the great Church of Rome is not indifferent to what is being done to further a better understanding between Christians of different traditions." Nor was Pius XI indifferent when he feared that the ecumenical movement would peter out in a neo-modernism. Pius XII had the wisdom to judge that the movement had eschewed that danger and that time was therefore ripe for a more positive assistance of the Catholic Church to separated Christians in their search after unity.

Chapter Nine

BOLDNESS YESTERDAY

IF THE present century is indeed giving permanent shape to Catholic ecumenism, the latter, however, was not recently born. Its history provides a thousand fruitful lessons, though some periods have not been very thoroughly investigated so far. None of the four centuries that separate us from the Reformation has been empty of attempts at bridging the abyss that keeps Protestantism far from the Catholic Church. A detailed study of those generous, if frustrated, efforts would throw light on what remains to be done; and one must regret that few historians have labored on this chapter of the history of the Church. Besides advisable ventures and mature ideas, such a study would also unveil the temerities of excessive minds and lopsided theologies. This would help modern ecumenists by pointing out between what numerous forms of Charybdis and of Scylla the apostles of Christian unity have to steer with no less prudence than boldness.

A thorough investigation of this movement would require the patient reading of little-known texts. A sure acquaintance with history would have to go with the insight of the research worker and the balanced judgment of the theologian. Since the over-all survey made by Tabaraud in 1824[1] our store of knowledge in this field has increased with a limited number of monographs. The present chapter accordingly cannot be more than a brief outline of a vast movement with innumerable implications.

As far as the approach to Protestantism is concerned, Catholic ecumenism began in the sixteenth century. It may even be suggested that it reached its climax precisely when the Reformation was not yet a settled fact. The Catholic reaction to nascent Protestantism would be strangely misrepresented were it reduced to the Counter Reformation that followed the Council of Trent. Before the Council itself the Catholic Reform was in full swing in some sections of the Church. One of its aspects consisted even in an attempt to persuade the Protestant Reformers to remain inside the Church in order to share in a truly Catholic Reform.

The men and women who have been called "moderating Catholics" or—with an altogether better expression— "evangelical" Catholics formed a group of theologians, prelates, and distinguished laymen who dreamt of reconciling the Reformation and the Church. Feeling the influence of Erasmus and his northern disciples like St. Thomas More, attracted by Lefèvre d'Etaples and French humanism, reflecting also the best tendencies of Spanish and Italian humanism, they constituted loosely connected circles. Lutheran ideas occasionally seeped through. Yet they remained in their majority loyal to the traditional faith of Christendom.

The most famous circle met in Italy around Vittoria Colonna and her friend Cardinal Pole. Cardinals Contarini and Morone were often seen there. Reginald Pole eventually drew inspiration from the views of this group in his short-lived reconciliation of England with the Holy See

[1] M. Tabaraud, *Histoire Critique des projets formés depuis trois cents ans pour la réunion des communions chrétiennes*, Paris, 1824.

during the reign of Mary Tudor (1553-1558). When he opened the Council of Trent as Pontifical Legate in 1545, Cardinal Pole affirmed that the Reform of the Church, had it been inaugurated in time, would have avoided the rise of schisms and heresies:

> Before the tribunal of God's mercy we, the shepherds, should make ourselves responsible for all the evils now burdening the flock of Christ. . . . It will be found that it is our ambition, our avarice, our cupidity which have wrought all these evils on the people of God, and that it is because of these sins that shepherds are being driven from their churches, and the churches starved of the Word of God, and the property of the Church, which is the property of the poor, stolen, and the priesthood given to the unworthy and to men who differ from lay-folk only in dress. If God punished us as we deserved, we should long since have been as Sodom and Gomorrah.[2]

The purification of the Church is thus the first step toward reconciling the Protestant party.

A second step consisted in expressing traditional dogma in conciliatory formulas that would have allowed Lutherans to find themselves nearer to the Church. Gasparro Contarini, the Venetian Cardinal who may have been the greatest Catholic figure of his century, chose that approach at the famous Regensburg Colloquy in 1541. At this important meeting, the Papal Legate Contarini talked things over with an important Protestant delegation. Melanchthon and Bucer were the chief Protestant spokesmen, and the young Calvin attended. This had no follow-up, however, partly because Contarini died shortly afterwards, partly because no agreement could be reached on the Papacy and the doctrine of transubstantiation.

The Regensburg Colloquy was the last attempt at a rapprochement before the opening of the Council of Trent. The influence of this Catholic Reform party is nonetheless

[2] Quoted in W. Schenk, *Reginald Pole, Cardinal of England*, pp. 112-113.

well attested, especially in Germany, by a number of tentative writings and proposals. Among the irenic apostles of that period George Witzel (1501-1573) and George Cassander (1515-1566) particularly stand out. In spite of exaggerations and inconsistencies, they devoted praiseworthy efforts to spreading the idea of a Catholic Reform with an ecumenical aim.

The Catholic recusants who found shelter in France and the Netherlands under Elizabeth (1558-1603) counted many a moderate mind who deserves to be listed among the pioneers of a Catholic ecumenism. Such was Thomas Copley (1514-1584), a relative of the Queen's, who wrote in 1569: "As sin has been the cause of this horrible schism and manifold heresies that now reign, so amendment of life may be a means to stay the raging course thereof, and to call us home to unite again, to the honor of God and peace of his Church."[3]

France itself seems to have been deprived of first-class Catholic theologians in the second half of the sixteenth century. Some politicians, however, tried to strengthen the truce between Huguenots and Catholics with theological discussion meetings. Thus Michel de l'Hospital, at the request of the Regent Catherine de' Medici, convened the Colloquy of Poissy in 1561. Theodore Beza himself attended and discussions had started in a congenial atmosphere when James Laynez, the General of the Society of Jesus, who led a delegation sent by Pius IV, torpedoed the conference. Who knows, it may be that the failure of Poissy, by wrecking the peace policy of Catherine, oriented her toward the blood policy that climaxed in 1572 with the St. Bartholomew massacre.

The gist of Catholic ecumenism in the sixteenth century may be reduced to this: basic concern for peace among Christians. Being child to a reform of life and to charity, peace alone can create an atmosphere favorable to the

[3] Quoted in A. C. Southern, *Elizabethan Recusant Prose,* p. 177.

hard thinking and the exchanges of views needed for a return to unity. For it was still possible then to expect mass reintegrations: the Lutheran Confession of Augsburg (1530) had been written with a view to a reconciliation with the Catholic "party." The fact that all the colloquies and endeavors of that century finally fell flat is no doubt due to the fanatics, who, on both sides of the newly erected fence, preferred open war and the use of violence to reflection and patience.

With the seventeenth century we enter an era, not yet over in some places, when the efforts of ecumenical thinkers are divorced from the aspirations of the Christian people at large. The "moderates" of sixteenth-century Italy had but formulated in theological terms a universal desire for a reform of the Church "in her head and limbs." The Counter Reformation having afterwards achieved, though in another spirit, the necessary reforms, ecumenism became reserved to specialists. At best it was in the hands of fervent and well-advised apostles, while at worst it gave birth to an aristocratic sort of theology only loosely connected with the everyday life of the Church as a whole, remote from the primary concerns of clergy and laity, and absent from the reach of their prayer.

In the first category we would place St. Francis of Sales, whose *Controversies* (1595) are far better and more than a mere polemical writing. They outline, among other interesting items, a theology of the Word of God that could well serve as a basis for a dialogue on all questions connected with Scripture and Tradition. In the same line would come the great Bossuet, whose *History of the Variations of the Protestant Churches* (1688) cannot overshadow the highly constructive *Exposition of the Doctrine of the Church on Matters of Controversy* (1668). Through correspondence with Leibniz and the Lutheran Abbot of Loccum, Gerard Wolter von Meulen, he assisted Christopher Rojas y Spinola, Bishop of Wiener-Neustadt, in lengthy negotiations with the Lutherans. This episode reveals him as a clearheaded ecumenist who makes wise distinctions between what is essential and what is secondary, between the realm of dogma and that of discipline. Bossuet and Spinola met with failure: their efforts had probably come too late on the scene, since Lutheranism was already hardened into a spiritual and clerical "orthodoxy" that could not be satisfied with mere disciplinary concessions.

A number of German and French works of that period belong in the same category of theological essays. Thus Theophilus Brachet de Lamilletière, a convert from Calvinism, spent his life studying the conditions of a reconciliation between the two faiths (1634-1654). Among others the famous Bishop of Bellay, Camus, friend of St. Francis of Sales, wrote an overoptimistic *Neighboring of Protestants to the Roman Church* (1640) and the German Masenius a *Meditated Concord of Protestants and Catholics in One Confession of Faith Extracted from Holy Scripture* (1662).

In the second category we may list some English irenicists who have recently been brought into focus.[4] The Benedictine John Barnes (1581-1661), the Oxford scholar Obadiah Walker (1616-1699), the Franciscan Christopher Davenport (1598-1680), and others endeavored to provide an interpretation of Anglicanism which would make it akin to Catholicism. This would have been, indeed, a praiseworthy attempt had it not brought them to leave in the dark, or even unduly to soft-pedal, some aspects of the latter! Better balanced, though excessively confident, were the impressions made by the Church of England on Dom Leander of St. Martin and the Oratorian Gregorio Panzini, whom Urban VIII (1623-1644) had sent to Britain on fact-

[4] Maurice Nédoncelle, *Trois Aspects du Problème Anglo-Catholique au XVIIe siècle.*

finding tours. The Puritan Commonwealth forcibly stopped all acting on their reports.

Between 1716 and 1726 an unusual exchange of views took place between the Archbishop of Canterbury William Wake and Messrs. du Pin and Girardin, Gallican-minded professors at the Sorbonne in Paris: they talked about no less momentous a project than a union of the Anglican Church and the Church in France. This episode remained totally isolated. No wonder: a few theologians could work out weird canonical and theological plans at their desk. But the Church in France had many other things in mind. And the Anglican Church, its Primate excepted, was not privy to what was going on. It was of more lasting value to a true ecumenism, because it belonged to the spiritual level, that a real friendship joined Cardinal de Noailles, Archbishop of Paris, with such a controversial figure as Count Zinzendorf, the oracle of the Moravian Brotherhoods.

To insure lasting results, ecumenism, as a matter of principle, must not be only the work of theoreticians working in the sanctuary of their office far from the massive currents of the Church's life. The ideal of Christian reunion should naturally awake pioneers. Yet if these truly wish to serve the Catholic Tradition and become part of it, they have to inspire the prayer of the Christian people, so that their efforts may be valid in the realm of speculation and research insofar as they are also fruitful on the level of Christian experience. A fully Catholic ecumenism ought to fulfill the expectation of the uneducated in the Church, to anticipate what the hope of the Church waits for, and to be carried on the daily prayer of the Church.

This popular aspect slowly reappeared in the nineteenth century, though it is far from fully restored yet. When the Oxford movement, after Newman's conversion (1843) was cleft in two, a Catholic section and another that persisted in the Anglican communion, the influence of John Henry Newman might have provoked a vast movement of prayers and initiatives for better relations between Anglicans and Catholics. A famous letter on the "union of the Churches" issued in 1824 by the Catholic Bishop of Kildare and Leighlin (Ireland) could have provided the basic charter of such an endeavor. Religious peace is the very foundation and groundwork of all reflection leading to unity. Keeping this in view, an ecumenical-minded person would have taken up the opportunity and done his best to pacify the minds of his countrymen. Newman himself was well qualified for this task. All his life after his conversion he fought a losing battle with the forces of discord that prevailed among some of his most influential countrymen, both Catholic and Anglican. Newman's endeavors were all but wrecked, however. For Cardinal Wiseman, through his sometimes phenomenal lack of judgment, misunderstood him all along. And Cardinal Manning, a great leader and a man of prayer, yet tempted by the demon of power, consistently opposed Newman, with the help of many a prelate who did not reach his own greatness. Catholicism should be universal not only in its doctrine but also in the culture that embodies it and the charity that presides over its daily life. Instead of this, England saw the provisional rise of an aggressive Catholicism, distrustful of everything that looked alien to itself and accordingly introverted, affirming itself in opposition to outsiders rather than through the spontaneous radiation of a centrifugal vitality.

In 1890 Lord Halifax casually met Father Fernand Portal, a French Vincentian. This was the start of a long intellectual and spiritual friendship that eventually led the two men to work together with a view to a future reunion of the Church of England with the Catholic Church. In that year—the year of Newman's death—the over-all situation remained unchanged, apart from the growing importance of the so-called Anglo-Catholic party within Anglicanism. It is therefore open to question whether the first efforts of Abbé Portal and Lord Halifax to have the validity of Anglican orders officially recognized by the Holy See proceeded from a profound wisdom. The all too clearly favorable view of those orders which prompted the two friends to action was likely to increase the unfavorable view entertained in other quarters. The further idea that this highly hypothetical recognition would hasten the reunion of the Churches also unduly mixed considerations of expediency with straight historical research. From those two points of view the question seems to have been badly posited from the first. Yet the debates that ended in 1896 with Leo XIII's pronouncement that Anglican orders were not valid proved extremely important through the backfire effect of this condemnation. For the rebuffed Anglicans evolved a more elaborate justification of their attachment to a Catholic tradition and to the liturgical usages going with it. They thus spread wider in the Anglican communion their understanding of catholicity. On the other hand, whereas the outspoken discussions of that period left the ecumenical consciousness of English Catholics largely untouched, they made the desire of a reunion of Christendom better understood among continental Catholics.

We have emphasized that a movement toward unity should, if it is to reach fruition, proceed from the totality of the Catholic public opinion, or at any rate find in that public opinion a slant through which it will become intelligible to the average Catholic mind. As history shows, several blueprints for union that were settled on paper with the leaders of the Orthodox Churches did not last, simply because they had no echo in the wishes of the simple folk of Eastern countries. This is, so to say, one of the laws that regulate the life of the Church. To speak in theological terms, Tradition not only includes the responsibilities of the hierarchy and the visions of theologians. It comprises also the hopes shared by the ordinary faithful. In all ages there have been prophets, lonely figures marching some distance ahead of the crowd; yet prophecies become realities only when the crowd follows. Here lie both the weakness and the strength of Abbé Portal's labors: weakness, because they were too remote, in their search for tangible results, from the slow development of the Church; strength, insofar as they prepared future opportunities.

Similar remarks, pregnant with more lessons of the same sort, must be made concerning the second spectacular episode in the friendship between Portal and Halifax. The Malines conversations, in which Catholics and Anglicans met between 1921 and 1927 under the chairmanship of Cardinal Mercier, wielded an immense influence in the form of mutual information and education. Thanks to them, men of good will on both sides were able to acquire a more accurate knowledge and to pass equitable judgments. Were one to view them as talks toward a coming reunion—which they never were to the mind of the participants—one should naturally record their failure. It was unfortunate that such an unrealistic interpretation of Cardinal Mercier's aim prevailed among Catholics of England, whereas mutual information was the only purpose of the meetings. Here again, continental Catholics, who had already been initiated to ecumenical ideas and methods, were in a position to view the conversations with more congeniality and to use them more fruitfully for the formation of a truly ecumenical apostolate than Catholic opinion could do in England, where the conversations were judged with severity and often with complete unfairness. The publicity made around them, however, rendered this reaction hardly avoidable. The vanguard of Catholic ecumenists cannot without damage lengthen to breaking point their lines of communication with the rear guard.

Exactly where they were unsuitably engaged, the Malines conversations nevertheless helped the cause of Christian unity. The role that the magnanimous Cardinal Mercier agreed to play in them came as a revelation to many distrustful Protestants. They saw that the Catholic hierarchy does not stand aloof. Its most influential figures keep themselves informed of modern movements of thought. They gauge the various positions of public opinion, and they are concerned with the endless storing up of prejudice and misinformation. Success is always on the retreat with the ungrateful task of the pioneers of ecumenism, who are always exposed to misunderstandings, who have to sidetrack readymade attitudes, to shock habit and laziness on the one side and, on the other, to slow down the impatient, to quiet the begrudging. One must refuse to count up its victories, for these do not belong to the order of measurable quantity. Its results have to be sized up over decades and perhaps even centuries. One will therefore avoid saying that the Malines conversations "met with failure."[5] These words have a meaning when they apply to schemes for union, diplomatic bargainings, or round-table debates. They are devoid of sense when the question is to evaluate to what extent prejudice has been assuaged and minds have opened themselves to the problems of Christian unity. Still less will one judge those efforts on the strength of gossip or press reports: this is a permanent danger in a century when sensational journalism has the run of big cities.

This chapter is entitled "Boldness Yesterday." The long period we have briefly surveyed is remarkable for the audacity of its views. Huge plans for union take shape in the mind of one man. Exchanges of letters over decades thrash out all theoretical and practical aspects of ecumenical projects. Theological discussions seek to heal the most profound wounds. Courageous decipherers try to read Catholicism into texts that exclude it at their face value. Authors wish to write the last line on all matters of controversy. Distinguished figures meet in highly scholarly con-

[5] E. F. Hanahoe, *Catholic Ecumenism*, p. 136.

ferences. All this reveals an eloquent vision and a striking greatness of soul.

Maybe all that was needed—and was needed over such a long stretch of time—to start a movement. We must admit, however, that we have become humbler. Our eye has better focused itself on the difficulties of the thing. And it is a fact that today illusion is no longer shared by those who see the problem of separated Christians as a whole; it belongs rather to those who imagine that all non-Catholics can ever be converted outside of a properly ecumenical effort, by way of posters or through radio and TV programs.

Hence the title of the next chapter: "Prudence Today." There is no point in blaming our forefathers for their disinterested efforts. Yet, "standing on their shoulders," drawing inspiration from the prophetic vistas they opened, we should take the exact measurements of ecumenism and pattern our prudence thereon.

Chapter Ten

PRUDENCE TODAY

THE PERIOD between the two world wars saw the beginning, in the Catholic world and especially on the European continent, of a renewal that reached all levels of thought and action. In the Catholic communities of Germany and France and in those of the smaller nations, Belgium, Holland, Switzerland, and Austria, numerous movements joined to constitute a real renovation. Although the less spectacular achievements of Spain and Italy should not be overlooked, attention may be focused on the productions of German- and French-speaking countries. They provide the background to contemporary ecumenical Catholicism. For the latter would probably not have grown but for the wider movement that laid the ground for it both among intellectuals and on a popular level. Today's Catholic ecumenical thought has developed, next to a theological aspect that cannot be dispensed with, a popular aspect necessary to its increase.

Writ large, one may reduce to six the factors that have contributed to the birth of a hopeful though realistic ecumenism in the twentieth century. The first four are partly constitutive of it, whereas the last two come from accidental happenings of World War II and its aftermath.

The *theological awakening* of our century is more important than anything else. Circles of Catholic thinkers, grouped mainly around the universities and institutes of French or German language, have restored Catholicism as a formative leaven in modern culture. Being sensitive to the various trends of the contemporary intellectual world, and sharing the hopes and disappointments of their Protestant or secular colleagues, the theologians of this day stand at the crossroad of two sorts of ways. On the one hand they belong to the great Tradition of the Church, through which they commune with the schools of post-Tridentine and medieval theology and with the spiritual centers of Greek and Latin patristics. On the other, they share in the gigantic effort made by modern thinkers of all affiliations to interpret our industrial civilization. The fact that dominates the modern world is that civilization has outrun culture, that techniques have left wisdom behind. How then is modern man to be understood? What some attempt to do with the help of atheism either in its extentialist or in its Marxist form, theologians do in the light of the Catholic Tradition now more and more deeply known; and their wish is to express their conclusions in terms that are intelligible today. The notion of unity is precisely one of the few to which man is now attuned.

Related to the theological renewal, a *return to the Bible* —meaning a study of Scripture that reads it in its historical context and its literary, philological, and anthropological conditioning—has helped to bring about perception of the basic unity of the People of God, of the intention of unity formulated by Christ, of the unity of the apostolic Church, and, accordingly, of the demand for unity which is experienced when the Christian conscience is faithful to the Word of God.

The *liturgical renewal* has also done its share to awaken minds to the mystery of Christian unanimity in the common prayer of the Church. The practice and the personal discovery of the corporate meaning of the Eucharist and the liturgy have spurred on an anguished longing after a gathering of all believers in Christ around one and the same table of the Lord.

Finally, the *accession of the laity* to responsibility and elbowroom, thanks to Pius XI and his Catholic Action, has opened the eyes of many to the extent of disagreements among Christians. Joint efforts by Catholics and Protestants with a view to achieving definite temporal purposes have laid bare points where sensibilities that have grown in mutual ignorance necessarily irk each other. Whence the wish to smooth them over through closer contacts in view of a more efficient collaboration. The persecution of Christians by Nazis in Germany and in several occupied countries of Europe during World War II threw Protestants and Catholics back on a common defense of the principles of the Gospel. It naturally provoked, as a consequence, a regret of their separation and a dream of unity that other countries do not now share with the same painful experience behind them.

Two new elements, that play an important function in present-day ecumenism, appeared in postwar years. First of all, the troubles undergone during a long war, the destructions, violent deaths, restrictions, and dangers of all sorts that had been daily bread for five years, gave birth to an immense *desire for peace* among the peoples of Europe. And true peace reaches farther than mere coexistence. It requires a common will to grow together. Forgoing denominational controversies thus becomes one of the factors that can create peace.

Secondly, the events that followed the war have placed Europe under the *immediate and permanent threat* of a new dictatorship, inspired by an atheistic philosophy. The dilemma of western Europe seems to lie in a choice between a Christian and a Marxist unity. For merely political, economic, or military moves cannot suffice as long as minds remain drawn apart by conflicting loyalties.

From all sides, then, the present situation favors the development of Christian ecumenism. We have outlined what answer the Protestant world is trying to formulate to that need. We now have to sketch the Catholic response.

In its doctrinal aspect, Catholic ecumenism today is part and parcel of the theological renewal. A multitude of theologians have investigated in what peculiar way the problem of unity is posited to modern man.

If it is undoubtedly true that the great doctors of the past taught a solid doctrine on the nature of the Church, it is equally true that their thought on this point is to be sought for in various tractates and is thus presented piecemeal, leaving the work of synthesis to the reader. Thus what St. Thomas wrote on the Church is contained in a number of articles and questions in several parts of the *Summa*. Now, one of the main contributions of modern theologians has precisely been to elaborate a full treatise on the Church, gathering together elements that were hitherto disconnectedly spread about in chapters on apologetics, on the mystical Body, on sacraments, on Redemption, and so on, and diving further into problems that were before left in the dark or relegated to appendices and scholia. This treatise on the Church, which is not yet completed to satisfaction, throws light on many a point that is of interest to ecumenical thinking. Thus the work of Father Yves Congar, O.P., which is mainly ecclesiological, has brought its author to commence wide researches under the general title of *Essays on the Catholic Communion*. Thus Msgr. Charles Journet has published the first volumes of a bulky *Church of the Incarnate Word*. Now, both these writers are also theologians of ecumenism. The former is well known for his *Divided Christendom* (English translation, 1939) which provides one of the most competent analyses of Protestant ecumenism. He has also published a systematic study of the place of the laity in the Church, a question that is of importance to assess the Lutherans' understanding of the priesthood of the laity (*Jalons pour une Théologie du Laïcat,* 1953). The latter is the author of an early appreciation of the ecumenical movement (*L'Union des Eglises,* 1927) and his ecclesiological synthesis includes many detailed appendices on the main Reformers and the greatest modern Protestant theologians. He thus presents the Catholic doctrine with a good perspective, showing the points where separated Christians have remained orthodox or have gone their own way.

Among the manifold aspects thus studied, the most important to appreciate the present situation of Christendom seems to be the notion of *vestigia ecclesiae.* It is required by fidelity to the Catholic Tradition, as well as in order to be true to facts, that we should consider separated Christians as being somehow, in spite of the negative aspects of their beliefs, connected with the Church, not only through a too obvious relation of opposition, but also through a genuine, though stunted, filiation. The Church does not abandon her children even when they forsake her. Thus all Christians are truly united to the Church through the theological virtues of faith, hope, and charity. They are also connected with her by the Word of God they read in the Bible, which they received in the past, as they still receive it now, from the Catholic Church. They finally share in her life through the elements of Catholic Tradition that they have maintained and the few sacraments that they practice, which are conferred by the Church herself inside Protestant communities. Such are the "remains of the Church" that perpetuate among the Christians of the Reformation a life-giving and sanctifying presence which is no other than the presence of the Catholic Church, the mystical Body of Christ. Whence the immense respect that every Catholic should feel for the separated Churches, not at all on account of their separation, but in view of the real —though veiled and impeded—action in them of our Holy Mother the Church.

With a similar concern for the fullness of the Catholic Tradition, other workers study the period of the Church's life that preceded the sixteenth-century catastrophe. Trying to know Patristic theology more adequately, they throw light on the common traditional elements that are claimed as their own, not only by the Eastern Orthodox Churches, but moreover by Anglican theology and by some sections of Calvinism and Lutheranism. In principle, the theology of the first centuries ought to provide ground for a dialogue between communities that, rightly or wrongly, believe in their own continuity with the early Church or affirm that they have recovered doctrinal continuity in spite of, or even through, historical breaks. The work of Catholic patrologists is therefore of paramount importance for ecumenism—all the more so as most of these are not only historians: they strive to unfold, in the wide field of Patristic theology, the points of view that will be most fruitful for theological thought in our century. Thus, among many others, Father Henri de Lubac has studied the social aspects of dogma (*Catholicism,* English translation, 1950), the interpretation of Scripture in the Church (*Histoire et Esprit,* 1950), and loyalty to the Church (*Méditation sur l'Eglise,* 1953). These topics interest ecumenical theologians no less than patrologists, since on Scripture, on the communion of Christians with the Church, on the corporate meaning of faith, there is plenty of room for Protestantism to deepen its understanding of Christianity.

We may mention here the ecumenical value of a renewal of Bonaventurian theology that is slowly taking shape. In scholastic thought Protestants have a certain acquaintance with Ockhamism, of the categories of which the Lutheran Reformation made fuel to no small extent, and Thomism, which they usually reject as a matter of principle rather than as the conclusion of a serious analysis. Franciscan Augustinianism, in its Bonaventurian and Scotist phases, is largely unknown to them. Yet some apparently feel that it could provide a spiritual atmosphere more germane to theirs than Thomism, in its modern hardenings, seems to foster. Several recent works may help explain the relation of man with God in a way that will be intelligible to the Protestant mind. In his book *Transiency and Permanence* (1954), the present writer has also thought he could be helpful to separated Christians who wish to grasp the structure of theological thinking, as the Middle Ages bequeathed it to Catholic Tradition. All in all, the thought of the Reformers, especially that of the first Anglicans, seems to have more points of contact than we know with medieval Augustinianism. An Augustinian revival in Catholic theology cannot help but favor a fruitful dialogue with the heirs of the Reformation.

Catholic ecumenism is finally engaged in a serious study of Protestant thought. Only a few first-rate works have yet been produced on the theologies of Luther, Calvin, Hooker, Wesley, and the other doctors of Protestantism and Anglicanism. Nevertheless we are in a better position as far as contemporaries are concerned. In the first place we should naturally list the writings that deal with the ecumenical movement of our century. Fathers Charles Journet (*L'Union des Eglises,* 1927), Max Pribilla (*Um kirchliche Einheit,* 1929), Yves Congar (*Divided Christendom,* English translation, 1939), and W. H. van de Pol (*The Christian Dilemma,* English translation, 1952) have compared Catholic theology and the positions of the great ecumenical assemblies of the present day. Others have brought into focus some aspects of Reformation thought and the relevance for today of the questions posited by Protestantism (e.g., Karl Adam, *One and Holy,* English translation, 1951; Joseph Lortz, *Die Reformation als religiöse Anliegen heute,* 1948; Louis Bouyer, *Du Protestantisme à l'Eglise,* 1954). Few studies of contemporary Protestant thinking have yet been published. One of them, however, is of first-class value. In his *Karl Barth* (1951) Hans Urs von Balthasar has given

an excellent demonstration of what a theology can be when
it has an ecumenical orientation, and he has prepared the
ground for a dialogue with the great Protestant thinker.
It is interesting to know that Barth himself has been influenced by the criticism of his ideas made by Father Erich
Przywara. This critical contribution to the formation of a
Protestant theology points to the exact task providentially
bestowed on Catholic ecumenism.

The now numerous books trying to outline Catholic
doctrine in a way that makes sense to non-Catholics also
belong to this general attempt at establishing a basis for
a dialogue. The works of Romano Guardini and Karl
Adam have their greatest value here.

Finally, another field lies open to research: the study of
ecumenism in the past and of the thinkers concerned with
ecumenical problems. Jacques de Bivort de la Saudée has
recently told the story of the Malines conversations (*Anglicans et Catholiques,* 1949), and Maurice Nédoncelle, who
had already studied the great ecumenical figures of Newman
and von Hügel, has written on some episodes in Anglo-
Catholic thought in the seventeeth century. There is room
for many more monographs along the same lines.

These works, researches, essays, monographs, form the
theological aspect of Catholic ecumenism today. It immediately comes to mind that it widely differs from the vast
projects formerly put forward. There is now no question
of working out blueprints for reunion, of inventing ready-
made formulas, of elaborating large-scale diplomatic and
theological strategies. What is being done is an infinitely
more exacting work, whereby the ins and outs of the central
problem of the reunion of separated Christians are little
by little put into focus. No one dreams of a new formula
for union. All are aware that their function is the humble
task of forerunners. We are now conscious of too many
psychological obstacles, and of too great a difference of
approach to theological questions, to hasten on with the

valiant hurry of Catholic ecumenism in the past. Provided this slow going is unceasingly carried on, its long-range results may come into sight at some future date.

It should be borne in mind, however, that the work of scholars represents only the first step in a program of Catholic ecumenism. The second step consists in bringing the insights and acquisitions of scholarship to bear on the concrete issues of the day. This is done among small circles where Catholic and other theologians have an opportunity to exchange ideas and survey their respective situations and problems. Initiated with the blessing of the Bishops, many such colloquies meet regularly, both in Great Britain and on the European continent. Though their contributions are naturally unadvertised, magnificent work is nowadays being done on those lines. It is indicative of a renewed vitality that the achievements of the elite of British Catholics in these circles are now quite equal to what is being done on the Continent.

The theological aspect of Catholic ecumenism is counterbalanced by a more popular aspect, which happily hinders its becoming enclosed within the walls of one school of thought or reserved to fashionable intellectuals. It may be here that modern developments are most significant. Besides theologians of ecumenism we now have apostles of it. In a brotherly association with the searchers, these devote their life to spreading the ideas and concerns of the reunion of separated Christians and to encouraging prayer for unity. Periodicals in most European languages carry news and explain principles of judgment and action concerning the present movement toward unity. In its own sphere each of them is indispensable. Still more indispensable, however, and as a matter of fact dependent on those periodicals, is the movement of prayer to which several apostles of unity have given their life.

It is often forgotten that Pope Leo XIII was among the

first who encouraged prayer for the unity of the Church. In 1895 and 1897 he advised Catholics to consecrate to it the nine days before Pentecost. An invocation to the Holy Spirit seemed appropriate to hasten the day of return of separated Christians, since the proper function of the Holy Spirit in the economy of salvation is to make us understand what Christ taught and therefore, among other things, His wish for unity. In present-day practice, however, this novena—which was still recommended, in the form of an octave, by the organizers of the first assembly of *Faith and Order*—has been usually pushed aside by an octave going from January 18 to January 25. Initiated by Paul Wattson (1863-1940), who launched the idea and put it into operation in 1908 when he still belonged to the Protestant Episcopal Church, this practice is also associated with the name of Abbé Paul Couturier (died 1953) who became its most dynamic promoter in Europe. Thanks to Abbé Couturier, the January Octave has become a time of prayer not only for Catholics, who hope in the reunion of all around the Apostolic See, but for many separated Christians, who pray for the "visible unity of the Kingdom of God such as Christ wants it and through the means He will choose." This week of the universal prayer of Christians for unity provides all with the opportunity of sharing, either privately or in public, in a common begging of the Father of every perfect gift, that He may bring to perfection the gift of unity once for all bestowed on the Church. Encouraged as it was by Puis X in 1909 and Benedict XV in 1916, this prayer octave is widely known in Europe and America. Yet its European form, which is due to Abbé Couturier, has made it a more ecumenical sort of prayer than its American form. For Protestantism cannot in conscience join in a prayer for its own disappearance, whereas it can and must pray for a better knowledge of the will of Christ and for the grace to fulfill it.

The most powerful influence on the popular aspect of

Catholic ecumenism was wielded by a martyr of unity, Father Max Joseph Metzger (1887-1944), who was killed by Nazis because of his efforts in favor of peace. Max Metzger was brought to the question of peace among Christians from his earlier concern for peace among nations. Having founded in 1916 a society, the "League of the White Cross for World Peace," that eventually became a religious Congregation, the "Society of Christ the King," he destined it to work for the reconciliation of nations and Christians. Twice jailed by Hitler's police, he persisted in his activities until a third imprisonment ended with his death. Max Metzger was among the first Catholics who understood the scope of the ecumenical movement among Protestants. Out of what was loosely called the Una Sancta movement in Germany—an unorganized getting together of Catholics and Protestants—he formed in 1939 the "Una Sancta Brotherhood." As an organization, the Brotherhood did not survive its founder long. Yet the movement itself, now supervised by the Catholic Archbishop of Paderborn, Msgr. Jaegher, is still the most consistent and continuous attempt to meet Protestants in a spirit of mutual understanding and good will, with a view to better knowledge of, and deeper prayer for, one another.

Should we list in this ecumenism of the Christian people the various groups that try to convert Protestants? The numberless *Catholic Information Centers* of the United States, the *Catholic Missionary Society* in England, in Germany an important *Winfriedbund* founded by Father Gisbet Menge in 1920 and several "Houses of the Open Door" share the common aim of converting non-Catholics to the one Church. This task cannot be underestimated, insofar as many self-styled "Protestants" are in reality unbelievers and also because there are true Christians in the separated Churches that feel in duty bound to forsake their denomination and join the Catholic Church finally recognized. This is not, however, an ecumenical endeavor in the sense in which we have described ecumenism. This part of the modern apostolate, which is indeed a privileged aspect of the mission of the Church and has great importance for the re-Christianization of our secular societies, is located by its very nature outside of Catholic ecumenism properly so called.

A consistent conception of Catholic ecumenism is implied in the efforts made nowadays to constitute it.

Shortly before his death, Abbé Paul Couturier wrote a short epitome of his views in a pamphlet, *Prayer and Christian Unity* (1952). Facing the two facts that Catholics are, on the one hand, in a theological position all their own and, on the other, in a psychological position which is shared by Protestants—since Protestants also are convinced that the opposite point of view is wrong—he concludes that for the time being the only possible union between Catholics and Protestants may be achieved in prayer. There is no question of mixed liturgical services: these have to be unequivocally condemned for they lead to doctrinal confusion. Yet a true union is possible, insofar as each side prays for the other and even devotes itself entirely and without reservation to the sanctification of the other. This is a "spiritual emulation" through which all Christians can remain faithful to their convictions, while they build up at the same time a community of prayer. The aim of this "emulation" should not be the suppression of this or that community of Christians—for a purely negative approach would create unity by voiding the problem of its meaning—but rather a growing together through which each will help all others to become better Christians, a "parallelaboration" through which the Church and the Churches would encourage one another to know and do the will of Christ. Such "parallelaboration"—to use a quaint term coined by Couturier—being the result of a prayer one for another that respects the loyalty of each and sundry, will create on the face of the earth a spiritual power of cosmic dimensions that will some day be strong enough to break through human pride and reintegrate all Christians in the bosom of the one and only Church.

In the context of the Una Sancta movement, Father Matthias Laros, trying to systematize the insights of Max Metzger, has elaborated a similar conception of Catholic ecumenism. His book *Schöpferischer Friede der Konfessionen* (1950) calls "creative peace" the ideal he has in mind. The creative peace which alone is able efficiently to prepare the reunion of Christians consists in making the faithful of various communions, and even those communions as such, no longer enemies or rivals, or even neighbors who turn their backs on one another, but indeed "partners" helping each other toward a more thorough and less selfish adherence to truth and charity. Three elements constitute that creative peace: a mutual *respect* between Christian communions, as part of their spiritual life and presiding over their practical initiatives; a mutual *love* between individual Christians and even different communions, whereby each and all would ever seek what will promote peace rather than what can become a source of discord; a mutual *exchange* of human and spiritual values. The peace thus achieved will be creative. It will naturally not create new beliefs, but a new psychological turn of mind; not a new Church, but a new insight into the requirements of unity. Through a sort of spiritual growth that may be compared with dogmatic development, the faithful at the time of this creative peace will be brought to discover practical means of joining together into one body. The function of the Catholic Church in the upbuilding of that peace consists, therefore, in placing the depths of her theology, the heights of her sanctity, and the experiences of her Tradition at the service of separated Christians. When creative peace ultimately comes true, she will have the final role of opening herself to others as the harbor of their wandering and the term of their desire.

As Matthias Laros sees it, the period we live in is providentially prepared to see the start of a movement toward the establishment of a creative peace. Admittedly, peace is no mere human achievement: it is graciously given in Christ. Yet minds are now better disposed than in the past to receive it with all its creative possibilities. What should we then do when we look up this suggestive vista of what gift God keeps ready for us when we are mature enough to receive it?

Laros sums up ecumenical activities under three headings. *Prayer and repentance* must be given pride of place. Then, the various communities ought to join in a *fellowship of intellectual work:* far from remaining on a highly speculative level, this would also mean engaging in the humble drudgery of watching over classbooks, radio and TV programs, movies, and the press in order to purge any text or script that would slant the judgment of the public or sin against Christian charity and, correspondingly, to assist every positive contribution to religious peace. Finally, a similar community of work would be formed as regards *temporal purposes,* such as a better organization of social and international relations, a better understanding between colors and races, a common positive defense from atheistic propaganda, etc. All the talents of every man may thus be enlisted in preparing a climate of creative peace that will prelude the final reunion of Christians.

The views of Couturier and Laros obviously converge. A "spiritual emulation" normally finds its place in a program for "creative peace"; and the "parallelaboration" dreamt of by Couturier will be the first fruit of the latter.

The present author can only join his voice to the advocates of the "happy vision of peace" that constitutes the ultimate goal of Catholic as of Protestant ecumenism. It remains, however, to add some precisions on the role that properly falls to Catholicism in this common task, to outline in what manner Catholics can contribute to establish a community of work between Protestants and themselves. In the light of the Papal appeals that have been studied, of the lessons of the past and the present ecumenical experiences, we now have to prolong the reflections of Paul Couturier and Matthias Laros in their own line, and thus to put into better focus the requirements of a Catholic ecumenical thought within the ecumenical prayer of all Christians.

We will do it with the help of an expression used by the Holy See: working toward a "promotion" of ecumenism.

Chapter Eleven

PROMOTION OF ECUMENISM

CATHOLIC Bishops can efficiently promote the ecumenical movement—as is expected of them in the Holy See's 1949 Instruction—only when the theologians are ready to assist them. As a point of fact, the hierarchy so far has been able to apply the Instruction only in countries where theologians were already engaged in the study of Protestant ecumenism. The hierarchy of other countries faces on the contrary an immense problem that admits of no easy or hasty solution: it has not only to train apostles, but first of all to create the intellectual environment which is strictly required for the birth and development of a Catholic ecumenism. In order to be efficient, ecumenism must be supported by a sound theological framework. Just to tell any available prelate or any religious or other society to take charge of the problem would be running into disaster right away. For this highly specialized apostolate demands, besides a profound sense of the requirements of Catholic truth and an unshakable loyalty to the Church, a psychological and spiritual understanding of the Protestant positions and sensibility. Christian truth is Catholic or it is not Christian truth. Yet when we have said that, we have done little to help truth to triumph and, according to Christ's promise, liberate men. Much more is to be done.

To a solid acquaintance with history one must join a magnanimity of intelligence able to perceive basic intentions, to follow developments of ideas, to discern their interconnections and anticipate their future orientation, humbly to rise above sociological conditionings in order to tackle the core of the questions and yet to grasp these in their concrete existential setting.

Catholic ecumenism needs a genuine vocation, which amounts neither to a mere theological culture nor only to a grace of state or—and least of all—to apostolic zeal, but rather unites them all in a spiritual and intellectual preparation to which a deep and self-educating experience is essential. Nevertheless, the theological structure of Catholic ecumenism should interest all who are concerned with a fully Catholic culture. Far from being some sort of private property, it is born of the implications of faith when placed face to face with the pluralism of our Christian traditions.[1]

The first step of a promotion of the ecumenical movement by Catholics consists in putting at its disposal the lights of Catholic theology, not indeed through polemics or even in purely apologetical works, but rather in disinterested investigations of the points which ecumenical developments have brought to the attention of Protestants.

The ecumenical movement being what it is, an effort has to be made to explain the true notion of the Church as understood in the Catholic Tradition. Protestants in general are acquainted with the conditions imposed by the Church for a return to unity. The trouble is that these conditions are too often put forward without the theological explanations that would make them intelligible. Through lack of method or indifference to a sound promotion of ecumenism, we thus place our separated brethren face to face, not

[1] For a previous tentative outline of the program proposed in the following pages, cf. "Reflexions on the Catholic Approach to Separated Christians," in *Unitas*, 1951, n. 1, pp. 9-12.

with the doctrine as such, but rather with the doctrine plus a presentation of it that makes it look like an arrogant and incomprehensible demand. What is to Catholics the humility of obedience to truth takes the proportions, for Protestants, of an absurd leap in the dark.

A theological explanation of this should bear on the following point: how can one and the same reality be at the same time, and without endangering its divine origin and its earthly components, the Church of heaven and the Church of the earth? We distinguished three planes in the theological setup of Protestant ecumenism: the heavenly level, abode of the Church as seen by God; the earthly level, where the various Churches, all of them imperfect and sinful, dwell; and a medial level whereto the Churches accede for a while when God's grace makes them better replicas of the heavenly Church. Thus William Temple, Archbishop of Canterbury, wrote in 1943: "I believe that all the doctrinal errors of Rome come from the direct identification of the Church as an organised Institution, taking its part in the process of history, with the Kingdom of God. . . . The only wholesome view is one which regards it as being constituted as the Church by the powers of the Kingdom of God within it and yet as being always composed of people still citizens of the world, so that those powers manifest themselves partially and fitfully, and the historical Church is a mixed body."[2]

According to Catholic doctrine, on the contrary, the Church here below is the organ through which the heavenly Church becomes present on this earth. Being infallibly assisted by the Holy Spirit and having Christ ever present in her midst, she is simply unable to fail in her mission. The human shortcomings that were largely responsible for the sixteenth-century break-up do not belong to the Church as such, but to the men her members. By explaining this, the Catholic may open hitherto unperceived vistas on the

[2] Quoted in F. A. Iremonger, *William Temple*, p. 420.

divine plan of salvation and on the meaning of the Church as the social embodiment of the sphere of Christ's activity. Even though he may not convince his opponents, the Catholic ecumenist will help Protestants to put things into better focus. The Catholic position will at last be understood in all its breadth, with the manifold consequences that are incident to it at all levels of thought and behavior.

Nearly all theological problems may be approached from a like angle, keeping in view the exact point where the Reformers lost track of the Catholic tradition. Not only Mariology and ecclesiology thrive better from being treated in this way, but Christology and soteriology[3] also gain from such an elaboration. For the interconnection of the mysteries of faith—what is called the "analogy" of faith—is such that modification on one point entails a slant on another. Once such a bias is introduced, to keep together the traditional vision of things visible and invisible becomes a task that faces impossible odds.

Theologians who do this work will be led to notice a certain correspondence between some formulas of the Catholic Tradition and some Protestant themes. It sometimes happened that the Reformers rejected a doctrine that they erroneously thought was Catholic, while they opposed to it a position which is basically or partly Catholic but is hard to recognize as such because it uses new terms and other categories. Where this has taken place, a way of approach must be cut through divergences of vocabulary that made past theologians argue at cross purposes instead of reaching essential problems. It is clear enough that we are all sensitive to associations evoked by words. We react to expressions before knowing in what sense they are meant. Thus the words "war," "proletariat," "revolution," "democracy" start psychological reflexes that are difficult to control. The same thing happens with theological parlance.

[3] Soteriology is the part of the Christian doctrine that deals with salvation and the means of salvation.

Consider the phrase "free interpretation." To the Catholic it suggests a doctrinal chaos where each would interpret the Bible to fit his own taste, nobody having authority to contradict or control that exegesis. The same words mean something entirely other to the Protestant. "Free interpretation" evokes in him the dramatic responsibility of each man who tries to be faithful to the interior testimony of the Holy Spirit when he reads the Bible as the Word of God. And this interior testimony is nothing but an assistance of God to the believer who reads the Bible with faith. If we look at it closely, this doctrine looks very much like what Catholic theology knows as the "light of faith," the God-given interior light in which we believe. If it is understood aright, an expression that was distressing at its face value can truly help orientate Protestantism in the direction of Catholic truth. What was a chasm of separation turns out to be spanned by a bridge. A patient study of Protestant theology is likely to discover many a point of contact where others stumble into controversy.

On his own part the Protestant will learn better to understand the Catholic conceptions that have been veiled for him by centuries-old misrepresentations. He will see that Papal infallibility has nothing to do with an intellectual tyranny, that dogmatic definitions are in no way strait jackets keeping intelligence captive, that this or that statement has not the sense he reads into it. Thus the notion of justification, of salvation through works, as accepted in Catholicism, necessarily presupposes the doctrine of justification by the sole grace of Christ, salvation through faith in the only Mediator. A denial of the latter, therefore, does not follow from an affirmation of the former.

Such a reflective and comparative investigation necessitates a deep acquaintance with the development of Protestant thinking. Catholics often lose the feel of the ground when they see how quickly Protestant conceptions evolve at times. The 1955 Protestant does not read the Bible as his grandfather of 1900 did. The famous "branch theory," in the form Newman gave it in the last century, is no longer to be found in cultured Anglican circles. As years go by and separated Christians control their ideas in the light of a better knowledge of history and a more accurate theological reflection, the Catholic ecumenist has also to revise his notions on the thought of those who have received the legacy of the Reformation. He must keep himself up to date, or else he will waste his time trying to force doors open that are not closed.

One will often come across points of doctrine where Protestantism has seriously lost its way and mere provisos will not suffice to set it right again. One should then have recourse to history and find out where and when the landslide took place. Thus the notion of Eucharistic sacrifice is alien to Protestant piety. An ecumenist attitude will consist here, not only in pointing out the true meaning of the traditional Eucharist doctrine, as distinguished from more or less satisfactory accounts of it that may have been superadded to the core of the doctrine, but also in tracing the ultimate motivations of the Lutheran and Calvinist attitudes. These were no doubt influenced by excesses or deviations in Catholic schools of thought toward the end of the fifteenth century.

Studies of this sort, that never come to an end, may make important progress possible in the Catholic-Protestant dialogue. The Reformation, to give an instance, rejected the normative authority of Tradition in establishing Christian doctrine. It took its stand by "Scripture alone" as the sole source of faith. Now, the great medieval doctors also thought that their doctrines were founded on "Scripture alone." As St. Bonaventure wrote in the thirteenth century, "Scripture describes the totality of all that has to be known for salvation." The crucial point of the doctrine of the source of faith does not therefore lie simply in a choice between "Scripture alone" and "Scripture and Tradition." It resides in knowing whether the privilege of understanding "Scripture alone" belongs, under the guidance of the Holy Spirit, to the whole Christian community (Catholicism) or to each faithful (Protestantism). When this has been established, the Catholic is able to grasp both the structure of Protestant piety and the main lines of development of Reformed doctrines. His dialogue with Protestants can then bear on essential problems at last disentangled from superficial questions.

These researches orientate theological reflection in directions that are favorable to fruitful encounters. They could greatly help the promotion of Protestant thinking in respect of the basic doctrine of the development of dogma. One of the functions of the Church is to make explicit, century after century, as is called for by circumstances, some elements of the Revelation that were formerly perceived within the wider whole without being explicitly formulated. When the magisterium of the Church arrives at the conclusion that, on one point or another, this development has reached a climax, it gives it official sanction through a dogmatic definition. Because they have lived apart from the Church for several centuries, non-Catholic Christians see dogmatic development from the outside, without taking direct part in it. They naturally resent the definitions of the last hundred years as though these were appendices artificially superadded to faith. Conversations on these questions are all the more urgent as dogmatic development cannot stop. As time passes by, the definition of faith becomes more and more precise and Protestants are accordingly pushed further and further away from us, through no fault of their own. Those of them who try and understand Catholicism at the present time have to achieve the enormous task of assimilating the conclusions of two ecumenical councils where they did not sit, two dogmatic definitions pronounced outside the councils and the modern canonical discipline. This is a long-range attempt on which Protestant ecumenism as a whole is not yet ready to start. The function of Catholic ecumenists consists precisely in drawing attention to the historical genesis and the doctrinal and devotional implications of this development of dogma.

Taken all in all, those long investigations are far beyond the possibilities of Protestant ecumenists, busy as most of them are with more immediate concerns. Yet the ideal they aspire to requires such an intellectual and spiritual effort. Catholic ecumenists must promote ecumenism through that sort of study. It will be a slow, obscure work, carried on outside the spectacular assemblies. Yet the whole future of the ecumenical movement that runs through the Protestant world may depend on it.

This outline of a constructive Catholic attitude implies a number of requirements that do not directly belong to the intellectual order.

In the first place, the task of Catholic ecumenists cannot be mere erudition, office work, or laboratory experiment. Because of his loyalty to the Church and in order to root that loyalty deeper, the apostle of unity has to entertain a wide range of contacts with Protestantism on the levels of culture and spirituality. Trying to bring to an end disagreements that are not purely speculative but belong to a dynamic experience of existence, he must acquire the feel of all the impressions, insights, likes, and dislikes that form the subconscious underground of Protestant thinking. Being conversant with echoes and reverberations unknown in the average Catholic experience, he can share in new joys and sadnesses. Far from forgetting the Church, land of his fathers in the faith, home where he has been and will always be sheltered, in which his roots reach further and further down every day, he can also catch waves, decipher readings, and translate messages that otherwise would remain unanswered. His vocation is to make the Church and the separated communions mutually understandable.

Catholic ecumenism can develop only if it is backed up by Catholic prayer. Let us practice the Pentecost novena as advised by Leo XIII and the week of universal prayer in January. Yet, good as this undoubtedly is, it will have no lasting results so long as these devotions are not inset in the wider context of a life totally given to the cause of Christian unity. This is why Abbé Couturier made it his life's work to connect these periods of prayer with spiritual life as a whole. In all communions Christians should pray, not against one another, but for one another, that God may sanctify them all. Calling each other to warmer fervor they will thus vie in "spiritual emulation" and forge a powerful lever that may finally bring about the reunion of Christendom. When the clock strikes for it they must not be found lukewarm. Or else the opportunity will pass by unheeded, neither Catholics nor Protestants having been attentive enough to count the beats.

For the same reason the present writer published in 1952 a small volume[4] where he endeavored, more empirically than systematically, to relate the prayer for Christian unity to the development of spiritual life. For one ought to expect, if the movement to unity becomes deeper and deeper, the growth of a true spirituality of Christian unity. It also belongs to the theologians of Catholic ecumenism to assist and guide it. The program that has been sketched in this chapter cannot reach fruition without the help of this incipient spirituality. True theological work progresses only when it is supported by spiritual experience. The contemplation of the themes of Christian unity may some day inspire a really efficient ecumenism.

On all these points the clergy in general bear the tragic responsibility of being all but entirely indifferent, of hardly ever explaining the concerns and ways of Christian unity

[4] *L'Angoisse de l' Unité.*

to their people, and of thus overlooking a great opportunity to enlarge their minds and hearts to dimensions where they can truly claim catholicity for themselves. The program of "creative peace" proposed by Matthias Laros should at this point plug numerous gaps in everyday life that make Catholic ecumenism a still rare thing at the present time.

CONCLUSION

THE LAST two centuries have witnessed a painful development that further entangles the problem of Christian
unity: the altogether admirable endeavors of both Catholic
and Protestant missionaries have increased beyond reckon-
ing the urgency and difficulty of the ecumenical question.
Quarrels that were formerly limited to a province or a
nation have now reached world-wide proportions. After
being confined to Europe, Christian disunion spread to
North America with the arrival of the first settlers. Missionary zeal extended it afterwards to Africa, Asia, Australasia. In the wake of Protestant preachers it is now developing in South America. There is now no territory of
any importance but harbors, among a more or less vigorous
Christian population, a Protestant, Orthodox, or Catholic
minority. As a result, the catechumens that are brought
to Christ receive also the legacy of divisions for which
Europe was exclusively responsible at the beginning. The
world-wide expansion of Christianity entails a world-wide
sowing of seeds of discord among peoples and nations.

What can be done?

The Catholic Church is in duty bound to preach the
Gospel to all nations, since this is her vocation. Protestantism must repeat with Luther, "I cannot otherwise," since
conscience must be followed—as St. Thomas teaches[1]—
even when it disagrees with the Church. May both, however, strive toward a reconciliation!

[1] *De Veritate*, c. XVII, a. 4, ad. 4.

The data of Catholic Tradition on the only Church of Christ exclude a suppression of the problem by watering down the doctrine transmitted to the Church by the Apostles, and the Church must uphold the points rejected by the Protestant conscience. Yet to rest satisfied with this rebuttal, with knowing oneself to be in the truth while others have lost their bearings, would also dissolve the problem without solving it. To grow accustomed to the existence of non-Catholic Christianities would be one of the worst infidelities possible. The only way left open is therefore to leave complacency behind and start work on welding together what is still separate. Remaining faithful to his own conscience, each should try to promote coöperation.

Better mutual knowledge is the first condition of such an effort. To know the others we have to meet them, to keep up to date as to the ideas, influences, personalities, books that give color and shape to the universe where separated Christians live. One has to master the scholarly apparatus and the acquired habits of sound judgment that will insure both the respect of our Protestant brothers and the confidence of our Catholic milieu.

Training is necessary. If the Church wants to put an end some day to the rifts in Christendom, one of her tasks is to prepare apostles and theologians of Christian unity. One does not start on such a work haphazard and happy-go-lucky. The need is for priests and laymen, theologians, historians, men of initiative and vision, whose generosity equals their fidelity.

In these conditions an encounter with Protestantism may mark the start of a period of "spiritual emulation" and of the formation of a "creative peace" among Christians. Thus a more acute perception of the mystery of unity already present in the Apostolic See will be granted us and the word of St. Ignatius of Antioch will come truer than ever: "Form all together one choir, so that, with the symphony of your feelings and having all taken the tone of

God, you may sing with one voice to the Father through Jesus Christ, that He may listen to you and know you from your chant as the canticle of His only Son."[2]

[2] *Ephes.*, IV, 2.

Index

Nihil Obstat: P. Olaf Hendricks, A.A., cens. dep.

Imprimi Potest: Rev. Wilfrid Dufault, A.A., Sup. Gen.

Nihil Obstat: Rev. Thomas J. McHugh, LL.D., Censor Librorum

Imprimatur: Most Reverend Jerome D. Hannan, D.D., Bishop of Scranton

(Continued from front flap)

among Protestant groups and the evolving theology of ecumenism.

Turning to the Catholic position, the author examines the negative attitudes toward ecumenical attempts displayed by many Catholics and the contrary view set forth in official pronouncements. Past attempts by Catholics for *rapprochement* are chronicled and the standpoint of the Church today set forth.

Having established a sure basis on which Catholicism can safely increase its ecumenical consciousness where it is already aware of ecumenical issues, or acquire it where it still ignores ecumenical problems, Father Tavard goes on to consider common grounds for unity. He brings out the many attempts at united Christian action being made in France and Germany and finally makes concrete suggestions of what Catholics can do to promote a "creative peace."

"When the reader has finished, he . . . will have been moved, if not to dedicate himself to the task, then at least to resolve that in his own person he will no longer form an obstacle to what in the final analysis we can only hope will be the healing waters of understanding and genuine affection."

—GEORGE N. SHUSTER